Homeschool Basics

Homeschool Basics: How to Get Started, Keep Motivated, and Bring Out the Best in Your Kids

© 2017 Tricia Goyer and Kristi Clover

Front Cover Design: Tricia Goyer
Publishing and Design Services: MartinPublishingServices.com

Published by: Thriving Homeschool Press

Names: Goyer, Tricia (Tricia Goyer) and Clover, Kristi (Kristi Clover)
Identifiers: ISBN-13: 978-0-9991903-0-2 (print), 978-0-9991903-1-9 (epub)
238 p. 23cm x 15cm (9 in. x 6 in.)
Keywords: 1. homeschooling, 2. homeschool, 3. education & teaching, 4. education theory, 5. parenting
Nonfiction: Education and Teaching

Homeschool Basics

How to Get Started, Keep Motivated, and Bring Out the Best in Your Kids

Tricia Goyer
& Kristi Clover

THRIVING
HOMESCHOOL PRESS

Table of Contents

Section One

· ·

Getting Started

Tricia & Kristi

Deciding to homeschool can be a big step of faith. Whether you are starting with preschoolers or pulling kids out of school after several years, at first, homeschooling can be a bit overwhelming. There are so many different curricula to select, teaching methods to choose from, and learning styles to discover. There's your own family rhythm to adjust to, and there are state requirements to figure out. (Yes, we do have to worry about state standards, as if finding just the right curriculum and schedule isn't hard enough!)

It's a lot to wrap your brain around. Add to that the pressure from family, friends, and even neighbors, all taking bets to see if you can pull it off. They have questions and concerns. They worry about socialization and about hard subjects like foreign languages and math. They can't figure out why any parent would choose to teach fractions or (gasp) long division when they could leave it to the professionals.

The purpose of this book is to offer you encouraging information about homeschool basics, plus give you thoughtful and informative ideas on how to get started and stay the course. We'll cover some great tools that will help take unnecessary pressure off, so you can focus on what is truly important. (Hint: it's not academics!) We'll remind you that the best type of homeschooling starts with the heart. And finally, we'll urge you to push all those fears to the side.

Together, we'll sweep them away so you can see the path clearly. It may seem impossible not to be afraid, but we hope you'll feel differently by the end of this book.

We know you can do this. We believe in you. We trust that homeschooling will transform your life, your home, and your family. Mostly, we believe homeschooling will truly prepare your children for the life God's called them to live.

How do we know? We've seen homeschooling work in our own families. Between the two of us, we have fifteen children and over thirty years of homeschooling experience … and we both still have more than twelve years to go! We've seen how God has led us and blessed us as we've taken this journey with our husbands and kids, and we trust He'll do the same for you.

But before we give you advice, give us a few minutes to tell you a little about ourselves and why we each decided to choose homeschooling for our families.

Once Upon a Time …
Our Homeschool Stories Began

Tricia

I first considered homeschooling when I met a new family at church. They had eight kids, and they homeschooled, which was new to me in 1993. I didn't ask many questions about the actual schooling part. What I did notice was their kids. They had toddlers to teens, and all their kids got along. They enjoyed being with each other. They loved hanging out with their parents, too. I immediately thought, "I want kids like that!"

Soon after, my husband, John, and I attended our first homeschool conference. Listening to the speakers, we were hooked. We loved the idea of making sure our kids got a godly education.

We believed the speakers when they said that parents could provide a quality education in less time than an average school day takes, since homeschooling involves more one-on-one, quality time individualized for the child. I started homeschooling when my oldest was four years old. At the time I'm writing this, he's twenty-eight. That's a lot of years.

After we graduated two children, John and I felt called to adoption. When our youngest biological child was in high school, we adopted a baby girl. In the four years that followed, we adopted six more children from foster care. Our youngest son is six, which means I'll be homeschooling for twelve more years! (From 1994 to 2029. I want to take a nap just thinking about it.)

I've discovered many things I enjoy about homeschooling. I'll share those in this book. But thanks to our adoptions, we also had a number of new experiences, including one we never thought we'd have. We had to put our four pre-teen and teen girls into public school until the adoption was final. And while there were many wonderful teachers and staff members, I was not a fan of waking kids up so early, having them gone all day, and then cramming homework at night. That was not fun at all!

I missed the bonding time, and I wasn't too happy about the attitudes and influences my kids brought home. In fact, the day after our adoption was final, I withdrew them from their public schools. I brought them home, and as I educated them, I discovered that homeschooling could work for kids who'd been in public school all their lives, too. It took a little adjustment, but now, we're all enjoying the benefits of homeschooling. In fact, my one-time public school girls now say they want to homeschool their kids!

Homeschooling isn't easy. There are days I question why I've chosen this path, but those days are rare. Instead, I'm thankful for all the time I've had with my kids. Time to learn, time to laugh, time to grow, and time to build strong relationships. I wouldn't trade that time for the world, and I'm going to enjoy every moment until 2029. Well, at least most of them.

Kristi

I loved the idea of homeschooling. I remember the first time I said aloud that I was considering homeschooling our kids. I was pregnant with our second son, and our oldest was only a toddler. I was walking a friend to her car after a playdate, and we were talking about the schools in the area. When I mentioned homeschooling, you'd have thought I'd dropped a bomb.

"What? But people move to your neighborhood for the great school district."

There it was. The first of many critical reactions to my decision, and I hadn't even decided yet. Fast forward a couple of years. We had our oldest in a private Christian Montessori preschool, and I was starting to question my ability to pull off this crazy homeschooling idea. The preschool was amazing. They had so much great teaching material and supplies, and their walls were decorated beautifully with educational and inspiring posters. My husband was a little leery of homeschooling, since he'd had such an incredible public school experience, but he knew my heart, my desires. We decided that the next year we would try homeschooling and see the impact on our family.

That next September when all of my friends were dropping off their kids and heading to Starbucks or to a gym class, I was at home with our four- and three-year olds, trying to homeschool. Now, I did what any logical person would do when they were just starting out. I bought a ton of curricula … for … my … preschoolers. Yep. I pretty much set myself up for complete failure right there. Not that preschool curriculum is a bad thing. It was the amount that I bought. It was the three or four hours I was trying to get my little guys to sit. That's what set me up to fail. My homeschooling friends kept telling me to just wait and not stress about preschool. I should have listened.

I managed to burn myself out. Instead of making learning fun and going out and exploring, I was trying to see if I could handle the hours it would take to homeschool them when it was time to do real schoolwork. Yep. Again, with my preschoolers.

Now I look back and laugh. What in the world was I thinking? I did manage to completely freak myself out and chase away any thoughts of homeschooling for a while. I begged the preschool to make room for them the following year.

When the next school year rolled around, I stuck my oldest in public school. We kept our other son in private preschool. This time I was afraid to homeschool because I was pregnant, and I figured there was no way I could handle homeschooling with a new baby. Ha! Little did I know how much easier it would have been to start off homeschooling with a new baby than to start with a squirmy toddler. (You'll notice that my section on homeschooling with a toddler is cram-packed with ideas, since I'm now well aware, after doing it three times, that it is one of the hardest times to homeschool.)

I'm so thankful to have had my kids in private and public schools. Oddly enough, it gave me confidence to see that I could offer my kids a more customized education, one that suited their needs and strengths. It also gave me a chance to see the family unity we would have missed out on. The year before we pulled our boys out of public and private school, I was driving to two different schools and juggling my new baby's nap and nursing schedule. I realized during those hurried carpool moments that my older boys would not get a chance to really get to know their younger brother. Little did I know at the time, but they'd have also missed out on getting to know the two little sisters the Lord would bless us with a few years later.

Homeschooling has been such a wonderful adventure for our family. Both my husband and I feel so blessed that we decided to give homeschooling another try. I agree with Tricia—naps sound really good when I think about how many more years I'll be homeschooling, considering my youngest is three. But I know that the Lord will give me the strength I need to keep going. And I expect to get more than a little help from coffee and chocolate on the hard days.

Are you ready to jump in? Are you ready to learn more about starting your own homeschool journey? You really can do it!

Chapter One

. . . .

Top Ten Tips for
a Successful First Year

Tricia

I remember the first time I sat with my friend Sandy to talk about homeschooling. Her teen girls were carrying my baby and playing with my toddler. My five-year-old son Cory was running around with her two youngest kids.

"So, I hear you want to start homeschooling," she stated. The aroma of homemade soup was bubbling on the pot on Sandy's stove.

I nodded. "I think we're going to do it."

"How can I help?"

I opened my mouth to ask some questions, but as I sat there, I realized I didn't even know what to ask. Worries, fears, and questions crowded in my mind. I was concerned about being responsible for my kids' education when I had no formal training. I worried they'd drive me crazy. I feared I'd have no time to myself. I questioned how I'd be able to keep up with all the demands of our busy home, like cooking and cleaning, on top of homeschooling. I also worried about my own dreams. I wanted to become a published author. Would I have to give up those writing dreams, too?

Yet even as all those thoughts flooded my mind, I was too timid to voice them. What if I shared all my concerns and Sandy urged me to just send my kids to public school? I didn't know how to teach or what to teach, and I couldn't imagine homeschooling all morning and having a pot of soup on the stove to boot. Instead of voicing all my fears, I asked the only question that seemed safe.

I cleared my throat. "Uh, what curriculum do you use?"

Sandy told me, and I took notes. I had one question answered. One out of what felt like thousands. I returned home with all those concerns—all those burdens heavy on my heart.

Kristi and I both made mistakes, and we know what it's like to get started homeschooling. So, we decided to start off this book with a bang! Newbie gold. This list is a compilation of our best tips for planning a successful first year—things you might not have known to ask. They are a compilation of over thirty years of homeschooling experience. We go into more detail on many of these topics later, but we wanted to give you some good stuff right from the start.

If we were able to sit down over a cup of coffee and talk about the most important things for you to know and implement in your first homeschooling year, this is what we'd hope to share. Wouldn't that fun? I wish we could all sit down together. Maybe you should set the book down, grab some coffee or tea, and find a cozy place to read this. Then imagine us sitting there with you. We desire for you to be encouraged and feel reassured in your decision to homeschool.

We want you to know and understand how to really plan for your homeschool year. It has much less to do with a lesson plan than you think.

The beautiful thing about our wonderful, loving God is that even though we cannot be sitting there with you right now, He is there. He's sitting with you now. He'll be there with you every day, cheering you on. I promise He's better company than we are. He has far more insight and wisdom than we could ever hope to have.

Before we turn to the tips, I want to reassure you, too. Worries, fears, and questions may crowd your mind, but with knowledge, help, and prayer, you can push them to the side. If you don't have any formal training, that's okay. Most homeschooling moms don't. We don't. The statistics show that kids of moms who have no formal training do just as well as kids with moms who do. And that's good news!

There are struggles, like not having time for yourself or keeping up with all the household chores, but we'll offer tips for that, too. Also, we want to assure you that you can homeschool your kids and follow your God-given dreams. We have! And if you do, it's a perfect opportunity for discipling your kids to do the same.

And now for the gold. Here are answers to the important questions you may not have even thought to ask. Got your coffee? Okay then, let's dig in.

Kristi

1. You need to know the laws in your state regarding homeschooling.

You can make an incredible plan, but if you're missing required subjects, then you'll be scrambling to check-off all the state's blanks. Every state has different laws. There are a few states that have no requirements. So, you just do your best and don't have to answer to anybody. In that case, you get to plan and design your children's education with complete freedom.

On the other hand, some states have a ton of requirements. If you live in a state like that, make sure you're organizing and shaping your homeschool year around their standards. But don't fret. Remember, Americans are blessed to have the right to homeschool in all fifty states. Be thankful for this amazing opportunity!

To find out your state homeschooling requirements, we highly recommend contacting HSLDA (Homeschool Legal Defense Association) at www.hslda.org. They have resources galore. They have information about the requirements in your state.

2. Don't compare yourself to others.

When we compare ourselves to others, one of two things happen. Either we get depressed and discouraged or we get puffed up and proud. Neither are great results, especially since: "Pride goes before destruction, a haughty spirit before a fall," Proverbs 16:18.

It's easy to see what others are doing "right" and judge your homeschooling day as a "fail." It's easier now than it ever was before, thanks to social media. Remember, the photos on Facebook and the pins on Pinterest are only part of the real picture. Trust me. As a blogger, before I snap a picture of my perfectly plated meal on our kitchen table, I clear all the mess out of the shot. As soon as I get my picture, I put sippy cups back on the table and move all the crayons back to where they'd been scattered moments before. Don't get me wrong, I keep it real online. But the photographs don't show all the mess—who wants to see that? We mustn't allow ourselves to get caught up in our false perception of what is happening in other people's homeschools.

Don't compare your weaknesses with someone else's strengths. Don't compare your ordinary life with someone else's highlight reel. Embrace your life, embrace your strengths. Embrace your day, embrace your home. No one has a perfect homeschool or a perfect life. Remember that!

3. Don't choose curriculum just because someone else is using it.

This is one of the biggest mistakes new homeschoolers make. They panic because they go through information overload, and so instead of making an informed decision based on their own children and circumstances, they decide to use the curriculum their friend is using.

Did you hear that? It was the imaginary buzzer I'm pushing. Don't do that! No family is exactly like your family. Your friend's kids most likely don't have the same interests, talents, bends, strengths, weaknesses, or learning styles as your children. And for that matter, you're probably not exactly like your friend. You may have strengths she doesn't and vice versa. What works for one family may not work for another. What works for your friend may not work for you.

When I first started homeschooling, I thought that this one curriculum sounded amazing, especially after seeing it used by several families in our homeschool support group, including one friend who was especially eager to share its merits. So, I borrowed the teacher book and attempted to use it in our homeschool. The key word there is "attempted." I was completely stressed out.

What I didn't realize was that my friend is very creative, and she loves DIY (do-it-yourself) projects. She can sew and successfully complete all types of complicated crafty things. Well, I can only do DIY if it comes in a kit and requires no more tools than a glue gun. I am a masterful glue gunner! The curriculum we were trying to make work in our homeschool was not designed for someone like me. Thankfully, I had only borrowed her book and hadn't invested the hundred dollars the book normally cost. I handed it back to her, hugged her, told her she was my hero, and looked around for something more suited to my abilities.

The same thing is true with our kids. Some curriculum choices are great for some kids but not a good fit for others. What's especially challenging is that you can even have children who learn differently within your own home. That's actually what makes homeschooling so incredibly beneficial to your family. You can tailor your curriculum around each child's needs.

Please don't think that I'm suggesting that you have to create something from scratch or create something unique for each child in your family. You don't have to reinvent the wheel. I'm a big believer in "gleaning and tweaking." If you see something that looks interesting and fun that someone else is doing, tweak it to work for your family or even for one of your children.

Also remember that you don't have to figure out everything alone. It's great to seek advice from veteran homeschoolers, but don't worry about what's popular with other homeschoolers. Instead, consider your child's unique interests and learning styles. Then, focus on what brings joy to you and your child as you teach. Doing so is what makes homeschooling energizing instead of draining. Mostly, pray and ask God to guide you to the right curriculum, during the right season of your life.

Prayer should always be the first go-to on your to-do list, no matter what you're facing in your homeschool.

We are going to talk a lot more about teaching styles and learning styles in Chapter Four and again in Chapter Eighteen. So, help awaits. Just remember that God not only knows about the challenges you're facing, He can also lead you to the help and answers you need. God has placed this desire to homeschool on your heart. He's also given your children to you. There are so many great curriculums, and, with prayer and research, it's possible to find a system that works well for your family in your current homeschooling season.

4. Don't compare your homeschool to public school.

It seems obvious, right? You might even be saying to yourself, "Oh, I'd never do that." But I guarantee you will. Why? Well, because most of us only have that reference to compare to. Unless you were homeschooled yourself, it's really hard not to pattern some aspect of your homeschool to the traditional school you went to—and you'll drive yourself crazy in the process.

Fear causes many new homeschool families to try to make their homeschools look as much like public schools as possible. Many are afraid that if they can't handle homeschooling, then they might have to put their kids back into either public or private school, so they want to make sure their kids don't get behind. Others worry about all their kids might be missing out on in public or private schools.

The problem with this is that it doesn't allow you to really tailor your homeschool to your family. Let me back up a moment here to explain. One of my boys learns best when he's handling things. So, I knew I wanted to find a math program that engaged his style of learning and finally chose Math U See. He loved it. In fact, all of my kids have done great with this program. But here's the thing. Math U See uses a different sequence of introducing math concepts than the traditional school. Instead of teaching kids a little bit of addition, subtraction, multiplication, and division each year, they focus on mastering addition and subtraction before moving on to multiplication or division. In fact, they have separate books for fractions and decimals. Key concepts are introduced along the way, but nothing formal. So, my son learned how to do really high level addition and subtraction problems before he even saw a multiplication sign.

I point this out to illustrate that if I'd been concerned about teaching the way the public school did, I wouldn't have been able to best serve my son's needs.

It took me about three years to finally embrace that my homeschool was mine and to feel confident in the choices I was making. We must rejoice in all the opportunities open to our kids as homeschoolers and make learning an adventure. In a later chapter, we'll discuss more about the benefits of homeschooling that public or private school can't provide.

5. Don't wait to have all your ducks in a row until you start.

First, you'll never have all your ducks in a row. You will never have all your curriculum planned perfectly. You will never have your homeschool room, books, and supplies perfectly organized. You will never have your schedule all figured out. And even if you do get to that magical place, enjoy it … because it won't last. Second, you can only do this homeschooling thing with God's help, strength, and guidance.

Don't be afraid. Trust your instincts. Believe in what you already know. Remember, you have tons of resources at your fingertips: the Internet, the library, your friends/peers, and this book. Also, you don't have to know everything to start!

I've always joked that you really only have to stay a day ahead of your children. The beautiful thing about homeschooling is that you are learning along with them—and you'll be amazed by all you learn!

Of course, we all feel the weight lift off our shoulders when we have things organized—homeschooling is no exception. Chapter Seven will include wonderful tips on how to get organized.

6. Give your kids (and yourself!) lots of grace.

You're not perfect. It's okay! We're not either. We are all sinners saved by grace. Just know that the Lord is going to use you right where you are. Show your kids what grace looks like in your homeschool. Share God's grace with them when they get frustrated, cranky, or lazy. It's good to share, right? Don't forget to give yourself grace, too. We are usually our own worst critics. Don't beat yourself up when you make a mistake. Instead focus on what you're doing right and ask God to show you how to do better in the areas you feel you're falling short.

It's very normal for homeschool moms and dads to feel as if they aren't doing enough or doing things well. Trust us. You are providing your kids the opportunity of a lifetime. They get to see your life and your faith up-close and personal.

Being a model for our children is both an honor and a responsibility. We want our kids to follow in our footsteps, but there are times when we cringe when they do. This is why it is so important to demonstrate love and grace in your home. If you mess up and snap at your child because you have so many things going on at once—as you juggle homeschooling and life—use it as an opportunity to show your kids how to ask for forgiveness.

If you feel like you aren't getting to all of the boxes on your checklist, that's okay. (We will be discussing this more later.) Know that, if necessary, you can circle around to it next year. But the way you model your faithfulness to God today will be remembered by your children for a lifetime. In this book, we'll help you choose what is best, so you don't inundate yourself with things that don't matter in the long run. God has a plan for your children and your homeschool, so give yourself plenty of grace.

7. Slow down.

Take your first year to figure out your style and your pace, especially if you're pulling your kids out of a traditional school. Take time to adjust to having everyone home together.

Your first year doesn't have to be full steam ahead. I always recommend that people start their school year slowly. Make your first day of school all about fun and only do a couple of subjects that day. (We'll talk all about some great ways to add fun to your homeschool day in the next section.)

I don't even plan for full days until the second week of school. I also usually take two or three weeks to slowly add in all my subjects. There is no rush. This is your school. Plus, I've found that when I do take time to gradually add curriculum, our homeschool year gets off on the right foot.

Another great tip I received when I was first getting started was not to commit to anything other than homeschooling for our first few years. No mid-morning Bible studies. No co-ops. No outside classes that will fill up your days and run you ragged. The less you have on your plate when you are starting out—and figuring out this whole homeschool thing—the better.

8. Know there will be hard days.

We're just being honest. Plan on them! They happen to everyone—first time homeschoolers and veterans. Don't be surprised when they hit. We'll get into some very practical strategies on how to survive the hard days (more "newbie gold"), but for now, just remember that every good thing is also hard at times. Don't let one bad week (or bad month) discourage you.

There's a reason why we have an entire section on helping you keep motivated. In fact, we'll be sharing about some of our hard days in Chapter Twelve. Even better, we'll share how we've learned to get through them. We want to be your cheerleaders in this process of getting you started and keeping you going with homeschooling. However, we also want to be real with you—not every day is perfect.

9. Be flexible and schedule breaks.

Life happens. There are going to be things that throw you and your homeschool a curve ball. Kids will get sick. You will get sick. Family will visit. Let's face it—life is full of surprises, some fun, some not so much. That's okay. The beauty of homeschooling is that it's flexible. Sometimes you can just roll with it and adjust your schedule. Other times, you'll have to take a break and jump back into school when the situation passes or settles down.

For instance, I had a surprise major surgery. I had no idea this was coming when I was planning our year. We had to adjust. My older kids were able to get a majority of their work done, but we did take a big break during my long recovery. And you know what? Our homeschool survived the bump in the road.

This is why it's a good idea to schedule breaks into your schedule. It's hard to go three months without a break. Plus, it adds cushion to your calendar when things change.

10. Know it's okay to skip things.

I'm a box checker. I love lists. I'm one of those people who writes something on a list that I've already done just so I can have the pure delight of checking it off. So, what do you do when you are using a curriculum that has a schedule for each week, and it's Friday, and there are still lots of boxes unchecked? I give you permission to skip those items.

I've learned to have great satisfaction with just putting an "x" over unfinished work. Somehow, if there are no empty boxes, I feel pretty good—even when things are left undone. You can always move things to another week, double up somewhere, or get to it the next year ... but don't be afraid to skip things that aren't necessary. Any public school teacher will tell you they rarely complete curriculum. (Not that we're comparing!)

Remember, it's your homeschool. You can also add what you'd like, after you've subtracted other things. If you're enjoying a subject and really want to take time to savor and enjoy it, go for it! Don't let those silly little boxes stop you. Curriculum is your tool, not your boss. We will share more great strategies for those times when you feeling behind in Section Two.

Hopefully, these tips will help you get your homeschool off to a great start. We want you to have the best homeschool year ever. In the upcoming chapters, we'll be sharing about many of our struggles and how we overcame them. We'll start with one of the biggest struggles all homeschooling moms face—fear.

Our Prayer

Lord, I know You have put homeschooling on my heart, but there are so many worries and concerns. As I think about the journey ahead, help me not to worry about all the years to come—or even the months and weeks. Instead, Lord, help me to focus on what You've already provided today.

I know it's important to think ahead and plan, but when it comes down to meeting all my needs, continually remind me that You have already provided me with the wisdom and strength I need for this moment. I trust You will continue to provide—thank You for Your provision. Amen.

Chapter Two

....

Getting Beyond Your Fears

Kristi

One of my favorite scenes from Indiana Jones and the Last Crusade is when Indy is trying to save his father's life. In order to do that, he must find the cup of eternal life. Unfortunately, there is a series of tests, and only after he passes can he enter the cavern. The clock is ticking.

First, Indy proves he's penitent by bowing low. Next, he jumps his way through an obstacle course by spelling out Jehovah in Latin. Lastly, he comes to a great chasm and knows what must come next: a step of faith.

From Indy's point-of-view, he's glaring down at a wide, deep chasm. If he dares to step out, it looks as though he'll fall to certain death. The trail has ended. All looks hopeless. Yet in his father's notebook, which holds clues to successfully getting to the cup, he read that he must take a step of faith—a BIG step of faith!

Foot held straight out, Indy takes a deep breath and steps off the ledge. Instead of finding air and plummeting to his demise, he lands on solid ground! After tossing out a handful of sand, he now sees what was unseen before. There is a path, a way across. He's not going to fall to his death. With renewed confidence, he strides across to the other side.

My Homeschooling Step of Faith

I experienced the same trepidation when I first started homeschooling. Pulling my kids out of public and private school, I was certain I was stepping into a deep chasm to certain doom. I feared what lay ahead. What if I couldn't pull it off? What if they fell behind a grade level? What if I didn't have what it took? What if my kids drove me crazy?

The "What Ifs" seemed unending. However, I knew that God was leading our family down this homeschooling path. It was God who I was putting my faith in. The unknown was known by Him, and He was calling me to take a BIG step of faith!

A few days before we officially took our kids out of school, I found myself on my knees. "Lord, You have to show up if we are going to do this!" A stirring in my chest brought unexplainable peace. God whispered to me through His Word, telling me He would equip me with everything good to do His will, as promised in Hebrews 13:21.

Looking back, I can now clearly see the path He set me on. Just like when the camera panned out on Indiana Jones and we could see the path crossing the canyon, the years of our journey have given me a new perspective.

What about you? Are you fearful of walking down this homeschooling path? Or maybe you're afraid of the school year to come. Remember, God will show up! Keep your eyes on Him and not the uncertain path ahead. Whenever we take our eyes off Him—whether in trusting Him with homeschooling or in any other area of our life—we will freeze up in fear. And when we do that, we miss out on so much that God has for us.

God's promise was clear, and He followed through. I was not alone! The exact path was still unclear before me, and I had moments when I felt I might fall, but I trusted that God knew the way He was leading me. He saw what I could not. And, when I dared to take the steps of faith, He made my steps firm.

God was the bridge across the chasm, and He not only wanted me to survive, He wanted me to thrive and discover His hidden treasures that waited on the other side.

And guess what? I have found treasure in daily moments, daily joys. All these years later, God has shown up every day, and I continue to invite Him to be a part of our homeschool. (He's even gracious enough to show up on the days I forget to stop and pray.) He is faithful to me and my kids as we explore His world together.

Getting the Right Perspective

Tricia

Growing up, I wanted to be a school teacher. I have a young brother who was very sporty and loved to be outside. But sometimes, if I begged very hard, Ronnie would sit inside with me and play school. My determination to go into teaching didn't change as the years passed.

On career day in eighth grade, I was able to help a third grade teacher for the day. I helped with crafts and read stories, and I loved it! I remember sitting in the classroom with a book in my hands and two dozen children fanned out around my feet thinking, "I can't wait until I grow up and get to do this every day."

Then I grew up, and I found myself the mom of three kids at a very young age, without a college degree in sight. At my first homeschool convention, I got so excited about teaching my own kids. (Really? I can do this?) I loved the idea of teaching them, but something else caused fear to rise up inside me. I'm embarrassed to admit it now, but I was afraid of my kids being nerdy, unsocialized, and—to tell you the honest truth—just plain weird. (Don't tell me you haven't had those worries, too!)

Often when people hear the word "homeschoolers," they think of awkward children who don't know how to connect with the real world. I've found this is rarely the case.

I used to have an idea of what a homeschooling mom was like until I became one. I thought of tight buns, long skirts, and homemade bread (whole wheat, of course). While that is a wonderful lifestyle I admire, that is so not me.

I'm more likely to drive through Starbucks than to press fresh carrot juice. I watch *Once Upon a Time* with my kids and spend more time surfing the Internet than weeding an organic garden.

My fears started to subside when I looked around at my friends who homeschooled, especially my friends with eight kids. They set themselves apart not because of how they dressed or how they ate, but because of how they loved. The kids enjoyed hanging out with their parents, and the parents seemed to be having fun, too. They liked each other, and it was so unique, I couldn't help but notice. I am sure these teens were still moody, rebellious, and rude at times, but they seemed to have a strong family foundation that I wanted with my own kids.

From the time my kids were toddlers I feared their teen years, and for good reason. When my toddlers threw a tantrum in the middle of the grocery store, people would often respond, "Oh, that's nothing. Just wait until they're teens."

I'm glad to say that, after more than two decades of homeschooling, all those fears were unfounded.

Because I dedicated myself to their education and their growth, I have teens—and adult children—who are amazing.

We hang out, we have fun, and we enjoy each other. Not that homeschooling is a magic formula, but by choosing it, I made a conscious choice to give my children time. Time to learn, time to share, time to grow together.

Sometimes people are surprised when I tell them I'm a homeschool teacher. It may be because I still look sane or the smile on my face. It could very well be the tall venti latte in my hand more than anything.

While homeschooling is not the path for everyone, I'm thankful for my friends' example. I'm also thankful that over the years, God has given me the right perspective. Our job isn't to raise kids who are cool or social or financially successful. Our job as parents is to prepare our children for the moment they stand before God, the moment their eternity is at stake. Our job is to prepare them so that, in that moment, God will open His arms and says, "Well done good and faithful servant."

Now, I'm not saying that you have to homeschool your children to ensure that someday they will enter heaven. Not at all. But when I looked at my homeschooling friends, I saw teens who had a real relationship with Jesus, and it showed. My perspective shifted from how or if I could get my kids to be "normal" to what I needed to do to introduce them to Jesus and disciple them to live godly lives for Him. Their hearts are more important than any curriculum, and it all goes back to what Kristi was saying about faith.

The step of faith that we take into homeschooling might just be what will prepare our children to take a faith step with Jesus. I'm thankful this has been true for all my older kids. Homeschooling for me has become more than just having fun and being a teacher. Homeschooling has given me the time and space to teach what I know about Jesus, His Word, and the eternity that awaits us all.

In the pages to come, we'll be talking mostly about the educational aspects of homeschooling, but we don't want you to forget the spiritual ones. If you seek God, asking Him to be in the center of your homeschooling, there is the possibility of raising strong, godly men and women. But also know that you will be changed. Like Kristi and I have discovered, you'll need faith, you'll rely on God, more than you ever imagined. You'll find yourself seeking Him for peace and wisdom, and you'll find yourself on your knees. The good news is that's exactly where you're supposed to be!

Our Prayer

Lord, I've taken a step of faith by embarking on this homeschooling journey, but a life of faith is exactly what You've always wanted for me. Gently remind me to lean on You even on the days I feel like I can handle things on my own. When I feel tired, overwhelmed, and discouraged, sustain me with Your loving kindness (and an extra dose of patience and grace for my kids). Help me to fall to my knees whenever I feel I can't make it. I know You can give me the strength and wisdom I need. I also know my kids will learn more from my humility and dependence on You than anything else I teach them. May You receive all the glory for any success we have on our homeschool journey. Amen.

Chapter Three

. . . .

What Homeschooling is Really All About

Tricia

The number of homeschoolers has grown, and this leaves many people scratching their heads. Is this a cult? Is this a movement? Is this a fad? Before we dig into the how-tos of making homeschooling work, let's talk about what homeschooling is, and what it isn't. After all, every good structure needs a strong foundation, and for us, a great homeschool is built by knowing the facts.

What Homeschooling Is ...

Homeschooling is an educational choice.

Many people believe that homeschooling is only about religious beliefs, but in truth, homeschooling is an educational choice.

People who homeschool see it as an opportunity to give their children a more personalized and effective learning environment. Public school teachers try their best, but even they will tell you that teachers must teach to the median student. Many parents choose homeschooling because they want a specialized learning environment for their children.

I teach my children at the kitchen table, and I think they're getting a great education. We don't have a dedicated school room, and, yes, there is a multiple student-to-teacher ratio, but those things don't seem to matter. Those things don't impact how well my children learn. My kids live in a learning environment, which means their education continues long after we clock out of our school hours. And, yes, I can follow my religious beliefs, too. I can choose to teach the Bible alongside math, reading, and science. For John and me, that's an important part of their education.

Homeschooling is a lifestyle choice.

Each homeschooler makes a lifestyle choice by going against the norm of public or private school. Some homeschooling parents shelter their children from popular movies, media, and music. Others choose not to. Each home is different. There is no one-size-fits-all when it comes to the homeschooling home.

Yet no matter what choices you make in those areas, homeschooling impacts your lifestyle. Often there is one stay-at-home parent. The way you shop, spend time with friends, and work changes because you're giving a large part of your day to your kids. That being said, there are so many aspects of everyday life that you can choose to be teaching times if you're creative! Grocery shopping and running to the bank can be great lessons. You simply have to be imaginative and realize your lifestyle won't look like those of most of the folks around you.

Homeschooling is a family choice.

Homeschooling impacts every member of your family, including the children who are too young for school and the spouse who doesn't do the majority of the teaching. Homeschooling should be a choice that both parents (if both are living in the home) should agree on. If both parents are excited and dedicated to homeschooling, their kids will often pick up on the joy of learning.

What Homeschooling Is Not ...

There are so many misconceptions about homeschooling families. Here's a few that need to be busted.

1. Homeschooling is an overprotective bubble. Homeschoolers don't leave the house.

Isolation varies among homeschoolers. Most homeschoolers are not stuck in their house all day.

My children have been involved in choir, music, and traveling sports teams. We travel around the US and overseas. We take our kids to the movies. We volunteer to help people in need. Yes, we are protective about what we allow to enter our home, but for the most part, my children are very engaged in the world around them ... and they do leave the house. A lot!

2. Homeschooling limits kids. Homeschoolers aren't prepared for the real world.

At sixteen years old, my oldest daughter started attending a secular community college, and at twenty-years-old she had her bachelor's degree in linguistics. At twenty-one, she moved overseas and now, at twenty-four, she'd teaching English at a university. The education, religious training, and real-life experience she received at home prepared her for life, both at home and abroad. My oldest son is married and has two children and is a children's pastor at our church. Homeschool isn't limiting, especially when we teach our kids there is no limit to what they can do. I've known homeschoolers who have become recording artists. I know a few who are engineers. One is an attorney. I even know two homeschooled brothers who grew up to direct and produce feature films!

3. Homeschooling is like running a fortress. Homeschool parents are too controlling.

Parents homeschool because they are attempting to provide a good education and a safe place for their children. Many also believe it's important to limit the influence of unwholesome people and unrighteous living. But most homeschooling family know there is a world of wonderful things to explore. Just because a parent oversees a child's education and environment does not mean they are controlling. Instead, many of them are just are involved parents.

I have close family members who are teachers. I applaud their efforts. Most teachers will tell you that the common denominator for student success is parental involvement. Involved parents tend to have children who do better in school and in life. Homeschooling is simply parental involvement at its highest.

4. Homeschooling takes place in a bubble. Homeschooled kids are sheltered.

Sometimes this is a misconception, but sometimes it is not. It's not always a bad thing for parents to shelter their children, but there are cases where parents go too far and limit nearly all of their children's interactions with the outside world. There needs to be a balance.

I don't let my young elementary students watch the same movies as my teenagers. I pay attention to what my children watch, read, and listen to. This may be considered sheltering, but I consider it discernment.

By practicing discernment, parents allow their children to grow in self-control and wisdom until they're able to stand up to outside forces alone. Sheltering them gives them time to mature before they are assaulted by all the influences of the outside world. Ultimately, the goal is to teach our children to make discerning choices themselves.

5. Homeschooling is restrictive. Kids aren't socialized.

Some people say that homeschooling is restrictive because children don't get opportunities to play with other kids their own age often enough. In part this can be true, too. My kids didn't get enough socialization with kids their own age during some seasons of their lives. For a few years we only had one car, and they played mostly with neighborhood kids or kids at church.

There were times when my preteen daughter sat alone at middle school youth group because she didn't feel included. There were days my sons begged me not to make them play community sports because they didn't know any of the other kids.

So we made some changes. We got involved in homeschool co-ops. They continued to play sports for years (and liked it!). In high school our home became the place where the homeschool basketball teams hung out and youth group parties were held.

My kids have developed deep friendships with others in the homeschool sports and church communities—friends they can count on. My missionary daughter leads Bible studies for students. My adult sons have wonderful friendships. They all had awkward moments growing up, but don't most kids?

Also, another thing I didn't expect is how much they'd grow in their friendships with one another. All my children love spending time together now. Yes, siblings are the best type of socialization!

6. Homeschooling is overwhelming. Moms must have super-power patience.

My kids get on my nerves frequently. At times, I've tried to escape into my bedroom for three minutes of peace and quiet ... only to have them follow me, pounding on the door.

Our school days aren't perfect. Sometimes my children fight with one another. They don't always understand some concepts even though I try to explain. There are times I wake up and have a bad attitude. (Or they do!) With eleven people in our home, it's a rare day when everyone is happy.

Yet looking back over the years, the moments of conflict pale in comparison to the positive memories we made, times when we've had fun and enjoyed learning together. Now that three of my kids are grown, we talk about our field trips, the books we read, and the projects we worked on. We have months and years of material to draw from. We are close because of the time we spent together— good times, bad times, fun times.

7. Homeschooling families are all the same.

When it comes to homeschooling, sometimes the biggest misconception is that homeschoolers all come out of the same mold. Just as each family is different, each homeschooling home is different, too.

Instead of feeling trapped by misconceptions, learn to appreciate the uniqueness of your children and your homeschooling home. Feel free to talk to people about why you choose to homeschool, and invite others into interact with you and your family.

Homeschoolers have a lot to offer the world, and we'll do this best when we help people understand why we do what we do.

Our Prayer

Lord, sometimes I find myself worrying about what others will think about our homeschool. Remind me often, Lord, that there will always be those who disagree with my choices and actions. I'll never make everyone happy. Yet help me also to remember that my homeschool is not about making everyone happy. It's about glorifying You and guiding my kids into right relationships with You and others. It's about helping my kids love learning so that they may be effective workers for Your kingdom. I thank You, Lord, for all the memories we're building day-by-day. May these be a wonderful foundation for our future! Amen.

Chapter Four

....

Understanding Homeschool-ese

Kristi

I love being spontaneous. Nothing is more exciting than coming up with an idea and going for it. When I was in college and living in Australia, my friend and I decided to go skydiving because it looked fun—and this was after spending the whole week scuba diving on the Great Barrier Reef. I love adventure. However, when it comes to educating your children, I discovered it's wise to do it for reasons other than, "That looks fun."

Homeschooling is really fun. There is a lot of room for spontaneity—and adventure. However, it is wise to have a basic game plan and an understanding of what your goals are.

Don't get me wrong. It's totally fine to jump in and start homeschooling. Too many people over-prepare and over-plan. (Remember my preschool story—that was over-preparing at its extreme.) Yet at some point you have to develop a blueprint for how you intend to teach your children...especially if your state has specific standards. It's also important to become familiar with what's available and what's possible in the world of homeschooling.

While having a plan and goal is important, learning about different tools, resources, and homeschooling styles can help you gather the things that will prepare you for what's to come. Here are some of the basic homeschooling terms that are helpful starting off.

Understanding "Homeschool-ese"

When you begin looking into homeschooling, you'll discover that homeschoolers really do have their own language, and translation is often needed for your first few years. There is also a unique language depending on the state in which you live.

In my state of California, we have crazy acronyms like CDE (CA Dept. of Education), PSA (Private School Affidavit), and PSP (Private School Satellite Program). Please don't ask me where the second S went in that last one.

HSLDA is also an important acronym to know. The Home School Legal Defense Association is an organization that helps to protect homeschoolers and our right to homeschool. They are a fabulous resource. We'll talk a bit more about them in the next chapter. Just so you don't feel bad, it took me about two years before I could remember H-S-L-D-A without having to say their name first to figure out their acronym.

These are just a few of the new terms you'll encounter when you first get started. I've been amazed by just how many acronyms some homeschoolers are capable of using in one conversation.

Probably the most confusing thing you will hear discussed are all the various teaching and learning styles. Classical, Charlotte Mason, traditional textbooks, unschooling, eclectic, kinesthetic, auditory, visual—and the list goes on! Let's dig in a bit and get a basic understanding of these things.

Understanding Teaching and Learning Styles

There are whole books devoted to breaking down the assorted teaching and learning styles. In fact, when it comes to learning styles, there are even differing opinions on what they are and what they are called. Just like personality styles have had different spins put on them, teaching and learning styles do, too. Let's touch on the big guns.

Teaching Styles

There are many of styles of teaching. We're going to discuss a few here so you don't go cross-eyed when people bring them up.

Classical

Are you sitting down? This one took me a while to grasp. Classical education uses real, living books and hands-on experiments to train children. Classical educators do not rely on textbooks and presentations. They believe in reading, thinking, discussing, exploring, and discovering. Yet they also believe this is handled differently depending on a child's age.

Classical education is broken down into three different levels, referred to as the trivium. The trivium follows the natural development of a child. Classical educators know that a six-year-old student will learn differently than a twelve-year-old student. And a twelve-year-old student will learn differently than an eighteen-year-old student.

The first stage of the trivium is called the Grammar stage. This is typically kindergarten through early elementary. These are kids younger than twelve years old. It is a time period when kids naturally acquire and remember knowledge, facts, and information. The grammar of geography is states and capitals. The grammar of history is timelines and dates. The grammar of science includes scientific terms and systems.

Children at this stage learn key dates and people in history, math facts, phonics rules, grammar rules, science terms, and more. At this age, children love to hear the same stories, poems, and songs over and over again. They don't mind repetition.

My friends who homeschool classically amaze me with the all the detailed information their small children can rattle off. This method of learning inputs facts that a child can recall when it's time to learn the hows and the whys.

The second stage of classical education is known as the Logic stage. This is where students start putting meat on the bones of what they've been memorizing. They are learning to think analytically and understand the why behind all the different areas of study. They are starting to see how basic parts and skills relate to each other, and they start to learn cause and effect. This stage is typically upper elementary and into middle school.

Rhetoric is the last stage of classical education. High school students basically put everything they have learned together and are trained on how to articulate their opinions in writing and speech.

There are programs like Classical Conversations that help parents teach their children classically.

Charlotte Mason

Charlotte Mason was a British educator who dedicated her life to improving education quality in England in the late 1800s and early 1900s. She believed that education must involve the whole child, not just the mind, and the role of an educator is to help a student facilitate his or her own learning. Charlotte believed in an atmosphere, a discipline, and a life. She believed children learned a lot from their home environment, which was the atmosphere of their lives.

Charlotte Mason knew that a child's discipline, or good character, was just as important as any other part of his or her education. She also believed that educators should give children living thoughts and ideas, not just dry facts.

Educators guided children in living ways by teach them to:

- Read or hear literary books.

- Put what they learned in your own words, which is to narrate.

- Observe nature and the world around them closely and carefully.

- Record their discoveries in personal notebooks.

- Memorize and recite.

- Create something of their own.

Charlotte Mason believed that all children are born persons and should be educated on real ideas through their natural environment, the training of good habits, and exposure to living ideas and concepts from the beginning.

Unschooling

Unschooling is an educational philosophy that believes that the learner should be in charge of choosing books and activities as a primary way to learn. Unschooling is interest-driven and child-led. What children learn blossoms organically out of the things they find interesting in everyday life or the questions they wonder about. For example, if a child is interested in ships, he might learn about a ship's design, study about ocean currents, and read biographies about ancient explorers. Unschoolers may at times take traditional classes or work on packaged curriculum. The key difference is they learn according to their own interests and in their own timing.

Traditional Textbooks

There are whole curricula out there that have the feel of traditional schools and use textbooks for education. Examples of this are Abeka and Bob Jones curriculums. They have just about every subject you could want available through textbooks and workbooks. Many homeschooling parents feel comfortable with this method because it is similar to how they learned. They enjoy teaching this way because they were taught this way.

Homeschooling parents who use traditional books feel content that everyone is getting the same type of education at the same age, and they enjoy being able to compare what their children are learning with what is being taught in local, public, or private schools. This method is beneficial to parents who do not have a lot of time to plan and who simply want to follow a curriculum.

Unit Studies

According to unit study author Amanda Bennett, "A unit study is an in-depth examination of a topic (space, trees, cars, etc.) that approaches the topic from many academic disciplines—geography, science, history, art, etc. It is a complete immersion into the topic so that the student will see things as a 'whole' instead of as disjointed bits and pieces learned throughout his education."

Why do unit studies work? While textbooks give snippets of information, unit studies allow children to dig deep in any given subject. Unit studies are good for families who like a more hands-on approach. Unit studies explore one thing while also covering Bible, history, science, health, physical education, and the arts. Often language and math can be tied in too.

Unit studies often use real books and incorporate projects and activities that allow children to truly explore the subject they're learning. Similar to unschooling, unit studies can also follow a child's interest, allowing him or her to pick out what subjects are studied. They can also be done by multiple ages at the same time.

Eclectic

Eclectic homeschooling is pretty much what it sounds like—a little bit of everything. People who homeschool eclectically may teach a few things from a classical approach, other things with a Charlotte Mason approach, and then round everything out with a unit study or a textbook. Homeschooling teachers pick and choose what they like most and what works best for their child.

Learning Styles

When it comes to learning styles, there are primarily three that you will hear about the most. There are different ways to look at learning styles, and some authors and researchers even have their own fancy names for them, but most of the time, you can still boil them all down to kinesthetic, auditory, and visual.

Kinesthetic

Kinesiology is the study of body movement. It was also my favorite class in college. A kinesthetic learner is someone who learns by doing, touching, or moving. My second son is a kinesthetic learner. He learns best when he is free to move around or touch things. When I read aloud to him when he was younger, I tried to make sure he was engaged in a task, like copy work, play dough, or Legos. It sounds crazy, but he really does absorb information better when his hands are active. We used to drill math facts as he jumped on our little trampoline. Sometimes I'd toss a tennis ball back and forth with him as we discussed school topics.

Chairs should be optional for kinesthetic kids. Standing up or sitting on an exercise ball work well. Couches, floors, and bean bags are also great for these types of learners. I giggle because even as a teenager, he still is always picking up things to examine them, turning them over in his hands.

I vividly remember helping in his classroom during the eight weeks he was in public school. His preschool had been Montessori, so he'd had the opportunity to explore and experience things with his hands. However, as I sat in the back of his kindergarten classroom, I watched all the kinesthetic learners squirm on the floor as the class sang songs about the different letter sounds. My son needed something more than singing (auditory learning) and seeing a picture card (visual learning) to hold his attention and help him learn. Don't get me wrong, he was still learning. Kids will still learn information when it's not presented in their primary learning style. They just learn things best when it is.

Auditory

Tricia

Auditory learners learn best by listening to others and to themselves. These are the kids who will repeat each letter as you spell it for them. They want you to read aloud to them, and they have hard time concentrating on just the words on the page. Auditory learners would prefer to listen to an audio book than to read silently. This is my learning style. Even as I read books I "speak" to myself in my mind in a nice, pleasant voice. We'd also rather watch videos where teachers are explaining projects than try to figure it out ourselves.

Auditory learners are quick to memorize math facts, history dates, or states and capitals when those things are put to music or even a simple chant. A great curriculum for auditory learners is Sonlight because read-aloud books are a key part of the curriculum.

Visual

Kristi

Visual learners learn best by, you guessed it, seeing information. This is my learning style. Please don't bother telling me something verbally if I need to remember it later. Ha! I am a firm believer in name tags at large functions. My ability to remember information skyrockets when I see it. I will never forget when I first discovered that I was a visual learner. I was in college and floundering in my anatomy class. I loved the subject and the information, but retaining the mass amount of information I needed to have memorized for the quarterly exam seemed impossible. I got a C. I think it was even a C-. Ugh! Granted, I was using my high school test-taking skills to try to cram for a college exam. I had no idea what I was doing.

I was determined to do better. I realized after the exam that I remembered the facts that had been highlighted in different colors in my book. So, I started highlighting my textbook and notes in different colors. I'd first run through it with a yellow highlighter. Then go through it again with an orange highlighter, marking fewer facts because I already remembered the yellow parts. Lastly, I'd go over just the last bits of information I was having a hard time remembering with a green marker. Before the test, I only had to review the green information.

Guess what? I got an A! In fact, I got one of the highest grades in the class. I will never forget the smile on my professor's face when he handed me my test back. He even said, "What happened?"

I replied, "I figured out how to study for your exams."

Figuring out my learning style changed everything for me in college.

Visual learners need to see what they are learning. Help them to see the important stuff you want them to know, and they will excel.

Overall, learning styles are fascinating. I think this is one of the amazing benefits to homeschooling—you can teach your child how they learn best! When my kinesthetic-learning son starts getting frustrated because he's not grasping a concept, I'll remind him to try to learn it using his strengths and learning style. So, we'll grab blocks or a whiteboard. I've even made him do some figure eights with his hands as we talk through things.

If you're interested in learning more about other learning styles, Dr. Kathy Koch has a book called *8 Great Smarts: Discover and Nurture Your Child's Intelligences*. I listened to her talk about the eight learning styles she's identified at a homeschool convention workshop. It was incredible.

Are you ready to have all this simplified for you? I know I was when I was in your shoes. Well, in Chapter Eighteen we go into more detail about how to best use your teaching style and your child's learning style to bring out the best in your child. Be sure to check it out.

Our Prayer

Lord, thank You for this homeschool adventure that we are jumping into. Help us as we navigate all the various ways to plan for our year. May we always remember that You are ultimately the Teacher in charge of our school. You designed us with gifts and talents to teach and train our children. And You also created our children with different styles and ways to best understand what we want them to learn.

Lord, give us discernment as we plan and prepare for our school year. Help us to discover the most effective way to run our homeschool and teach our children. Thank You, Father, for always being our source of wisdom. Amen.

Chapter Five

·························

Homeschool Communities: Getting Yourself Connected and Educated

Kristi

It's really easy to feel alone and isolated when you homeschool, especially when you're first starting. It feels like you're taking the road less traveled. Well, you are. If you are like most homeschooling families, you don't yet have a homeschool community surrounding you when you begin. Sometimes you may be the only person you know who is going to be homeschooling their children. Okay, I was really tempted to say "the only person crazy enough to homeschool." Ha! I'm labeling myself there, too. It does take a certain amount of "crazy"—or should we say gumption—to get off the normal educational track that society prescribes and begin educating your own children.

Finding a homeschool community is really important. We'll cover all the reasons in the next section. For now, let me encourage you not to wait, because sometimes, talking to a real-life, fellow homeschooler is better than any blog post or book.

What I found interesting when I was starting to get serious about homeschooling was that as we told people about our interest in homeschooling, we began to hear about other families who homeschooled. It was like a secret world was suddenly revealed. I had one friend who had no interest in homeschooling but had a family member who had been homeschooling for years. She put me in contact with her, and that connection was just what I needed.

I also Googled homeschool groups in my area and found one. Amazingly enough, before I ever contacted anyone from that group, I met a few members at the park. I had my two preschool boys with me at the park during school hours, and we saw some school-aged boys playing. They were so sweet and polite as they included my boys in their game. I think I threw them off a bit when I asked them if they were homeschooled and then, when they said yes, asked where their moms were. It was all I could do not to sprint over to the moms when the boys pointed them out. These two moms were not only in the group I was thinking about joining, they were leaders in the group and became wonderful encouragers and resources for me.

Another great place to find fellow homeschool families is at church—maybe not your church, but other churches in the area. Call women's ministry groups and see if they either have a homeschool support group or if they know any homeschool families.

Last, but not least, another great place to find support is online. Blogs, Facebook groups, Pinterest boards, and live streaming apps (like on Periscope and Facebook Live) are great places to connect with other homeschoolers. There are a lot of ways to find us "crazy" people who have chosen that road less traveled. Be sure to get plugged in.

How to Navigate a Homeschool Convention

One of my number one recommendations for new homeschool families or those who are interested in homeschooling is to attend a homeschool convention. Homeschool conventions are a great place to get inspired, learn new things, find some fresh ideas, buy your assorted curricula, and be reminded that you are not alone on this homeschool journey.

Inspiration is what we all crave as homeschool moms, especially around March. That's about the time I start to hit the are-we-done-yet wall. Not so much my kids as me. Not that my kids aren't ready to be done, but I'm the one who's tired and struggling to finish the year strong.

Homeschool conventions are often just what we need to get rejuvenated. I'm known as a convention junkie by my friends. I actually attended three one year, all within a few weeks of each other.

However, attending your first convention can be a bit overwhelming. In fact, I found conventions to be daunting my first few years of homeschooling. Information and curricula overload! Now that I'm settled into my homeschool routine and needs, I simply enjoy attending the great lectures and seeing what's new in the exhibit hall.

Conventions are a great place to get your questions answered. Whether you are new to homeschooling or have been at it for a while, you often end up wondering if there are ways you can tweak things within your homeschool.

Let's admit it, there are times we all want to scream, "Help!"

So, listening to a veteran homeschool speaker can provide just the inspiration or advice you need.

There are always subjects we either don't particularly like or aren't particularly strong in. Conventions are great at helping us find tools and the tips we need to overcome our weaknesses. Sometimes it's great just to get advice on how to handle homeschooling with preschoolers or how to keep records (if your state requires it).

Conventions are a great idea, no matter your needs or your stage of homeschooling.

Figuring Out Which Workshops to Attend

The long list of wonderful speakers can be overwhelming, especially at large conventions. So many great lectures all in the same time slot. I've found the best way to solve this problem is to print up a workshop grid and circle all the lectures I want to attend. Sometimes I'll even go to the speaker's website and look around. Most conventions record all the sessions, so I usually try to figure out which one I'm going to sit in on and which ones I'll purchase a CD for. Sometimes I decide based on whether I think there will be visuals in the presentation.

Don't forget to pray over your time at the conference. Pray that God will lead you to the resources and lectures that will best help and bless your homeschool. God is interested in every aspect of your homeschool. I sometimes forget to slow down and pray over my decisions for each year. Homeschool conventions are a great time to start involving the Lord in your planning.

Navigating the Exhibit Hall

Books, books, and more books. My mind spun at the onslaught of choices when I walked into my first homeschool convention. I keep thinking, "I need that! And that! And that!" Although there are so many great lectures to attend, you will want to allot time to explore the exhibit hall.

Exhibit halls can be overwhelming, especially at bigger conventions. You may want a game plan when it comes to an exhibit hall. I usually try to have my course of study figured out before I go to a convention and bring it with me. Oops! Did I just speak a little homeschool-ese? Sorry about that. We'll talk more about how to create a course of study later. For now, just know that a course of study is a list of all the subjects you will teach and the books, curricula, and materials you will use to teach them. Having a list of what I need helps keep me from overspending. Of course, you may be going to the convention to figure out your course of study—and that's fine too!

Want a little inside scoop on what to bring with you to a homeschool convention? The number one thing I recommend for people to bring is a backpack with wheels! You will be getting lots of catalogs and possibly books. Carrying all this gets tiring without wheels. Some people even have small suitcases with wheels. You'll also want to bring a notebook and pen to take notes.

And now for a money-saving tip. An exhibit hall for a homeschool mom is much like a candy store for a kid. So many things, so little time—and money. Like too much candy is bad for our healthy diets, overspending, even on homeschool curricula, is bad for our financial diets. As we try to honor God with our homeschools, we have to remember to honor God with our finances, too.

My best tip for avoiding impulse buying is to only purchase items that are on a pre-determined list of things you really need. I use my notebook to take notes on all the things that sound like fun and would be enriching for my homeschool—books, games, etc. I make a note of which exhibit I found each particular item at so I can find it again if I decide to buy it. I give myself a night to think and pray about whether I really should buy those things, and when I'm home I also check prices online to see if I can find the items elsewhere for less or if the books are available at my library.

It is important to mention that your first few years of homeschooling will sometimes be your most expensive, since you will be investing in curricula that will hopefully last you a few years. This especially comes into play when your younger kids are able to use the same books in future years.

Whether you find other homeschoolers online, meet them at church, or rub shoulders with them at conventions, you don't have to pull off this homeschooling thing alone. It might take some searching, but we are out there—crazy families who have chosen the road less traveled. Believe it or not, as other parents around you see you taking your big step of faith, they might just feel bold enough to take their own.

Our Prayer

Lord, it's so easy to feel alone when I'm homeschooling. Lord, help me to see that with You, I'm never really alone. Please bring other homeschool families around our family for fellowship and encouragement. Help us to be just as much of a blessing to other families as I know they will be to ours.

Thank You, Lord, that although we are walking down the path less taken, we are still treading on a well-worn trail that has been navigated by many before us. Thank You for guiding our way. Amen.

. . . .

Chapter Six

Shaping and Planning Your Homeschool Year

Kristi

I will never forget my second year homeschooling. I was so excited to have a whole summer to plan out the year. The previous year, we'd pulled our kids out of the public school eight weeks into the school year. So, I was pretty much winging it our first year. But this time, it was going to be different. I had a plan to make a plan.

I did what so many homeschool moms do and bought a teacher's planner. I spent weeks and countless hours writing in our plan for each day. Yep! This year was going to be smoother, and we were going to get so much more done.

Well, my little "perfect homeschool year" bubble was burst after our first week. We had gotten off our schedule already. I was erasing and rewriting like crazy. I was so frustrated. All that hard work for nothing. By week three, I ditched the planner and went back to winging it.

Don't get me wrong. I love planning our homeschool year. Remember, I'm one of those crazy people who likes checking boxes. However, through the years, I've discovered better systems of getting things done.

Before we jump in, it's important to first think about how we want to shape our homeschool year.

Shaping Your Homeschool Year

Tricia

As a homeschooling mom for twenty plus years (with plenty of years to go), I have a lot of stuff. Books, papers, DVDs, CDs, schedules, you name it. It has been hard for me to choose what is best for our homeschool because there are so many great books and curriculum. Sometimes the choices become too much, and I almost become paralyzed trying to make a decision.

Yet even more overwhelming than organizing all that stuff is organizing our thoughts and our plans. There are so many activities, curricula, and subjects to study, how does a person decide?

For many of our homeschooling years, I filled our schedule with too many activities, too many subjects, too many boxes to check. It's easy to do. First, I'd add in an art class because it sounded fun. Then I'd agree to allow my kids be part of a drama club. I would also schedule in field trips and set up times to do Science projects with homeschooling friends. Pretty soon our schedule was full, we were all exhausted, and none of our most important work was getting done.

Thankfully, there was a moment when I stepped back, took a good look, firmed up what I wanted to achieve in our homeschool, and then filled our schedule from there.

Want to know what prompted that change? Genesis One.

I remembered that we are made in the image of God. God created the world with a sense of order, and He designed us to do the same. As homeschooling moms, we shape, form, and create our homeschooling world. In order to succeed we have to ask the right question. Not, "What do I need to do?" Rather, "How did God do it?" In the Creation story, God's wisdom is displayed.

First God formed. Then He filled!

In the first three days, God established supportive systems necessary for life and man's existence. He created the heavens and the earth. He separated the waters from the land. He made the stars and sun. He formed the framework that would sustain His creation.

The second three days, God filled. He filled His created world with plants, flowers, animals, and man.

- Formed: Day One = Created light, formed heavens and earth

- Filled: Day Four = Filled the heavens with sun, moon, and stars

- Formed: Day Two = Separated water and sky

- Filled: Day Five = Filled both with fish and birds

- Formed: Day Three = Formed land and vegetation

- Filled: Day Six = Filled land with animals and man

The problem comes in our homeschooling when we fill our school days before we build a structure around our schedules, our work, and our relationships. We make decisions out of emotions or desires without contemplating how they will impact our families. Nothing good ever happens by accident. If you want something good to happen in your homeschool, you need to structure your school carefully.

Here are some good FORMING questions to ask:

- Why do I homeschool?

- Ten years from now, what would I consider success?

- What values do I want my children to have when they complete their schooling?

- What would a great homeschooling day look like?

- Here are some FILLING questions:

- What am I doing that will help me achieve my homeschool dreams?

- What activities are benefiting my dreams?

- What activities are hindering my dreams?

- Where do I need help?

- How can I fill this need?

- What works in my schedule?

- What do I need to cut?

- What do I need to add?

The forming isn't something you can firm up overnight, and the filling will flow with the seasons. Even though some of the answers will change as you develop your homeschool, I urge you to consider the questions. I've created a printable to help you. You'll find a link to it in the resource section of this book.

I still have plenty of homeschooling years ahead of me, yet I've already graduated three of my kids. Looking back, I'm so glad I took the time to gaze ahead and make plans for our homeschooling journey.

Learning to form your homeschool days—and years—takes time.

It's much easier to fill them than it is to step back and be deliberate about what we allow into our schedules. However, it's so worth it. I know that with God's help, success can be found for my remaining homeschooling years ... and yours!

Planning Out Your Homeschool Year

Kristi

One of the questions I usually get asked when I discuss homeschooling is, "How do you know that you aren't missing something as you teach?" My answer: "Good planning!"

Yes, there are lists out there that show you what public schools teach each year. But we are running our own schools. As you saw in our "Top 10 Tips" section, one of our tips for homeschoolers is to stop trying to make your homeschool look like the public schools. Homeschooling allows you flexibility and creativity. You get to tailor your child's education to meet their individual needs and gifting. It's amazing!

Every year, I create a course of study, which outlines the direction I plan to take for the year. It's my basic road map to what my family will be studying for the year.

When you carefully create a course of study, you'll feel confident you are covering everything that you are either required to cover or desire to cover in your homeschool year. A course of study also helps you to identify any gaps or overlaps in what you're planning to teach. You get a quick overview of all that you may be doing. I say may because your course of study is your game plan, not your checklist. It's important to note that you don't have to teach every subject, especially not all at the same time. This is where that "forming and filling" work that Tricia talked about will come in handy.

To design your own course of study, simply write out all the different subjects that will be taught. My subject list includes:

- Bible and Character

- Language Arts: Literature/Reading Lists, Phonics, Grammar, Penmanship, Writing, Spelling, Vocabulary, and sometimes, Latin

61

- Math

- Science

- Social Studies: History and Geography

- Fine Arts: Visual and Music

- Foreign Language

- Health: Nutrition, Safety, and Personal Hygiene

- Physical Education

After you design your subject list, write each child's name under each subject, then start filling in what you plan to use to teach each subject to each child. So, if I have special math games or manipulatives, then I add those to the list.

Using a course of study helps me tremendously when I'm doing unit studies, too. We love unit studies. Having all the subjects I plan to teach listed out on my course of study helps me see what subjects are being covered by our unit study. It's fun trying to think of ideas to tie various subjects into our theme for our unit study.

No matter what state you are homeschooling in, and no matter what style of teaching you have, creating a course of study gives you a snapshot of your school year. Knowing my larger goal I also can be more flexible with my days. For example, I may teach science every other month, and history on the opposite months. Sometimes, I pick certain days to do specific subjects:

- Mondays and Wednesdays: History

- Tuesdays and Thursdays: Science

- Fridays: Art

If you'd like to see a sample of one of my past courses of study—and how I organize our subjects—I have a video that shows one and goes into more detail. I also have a lesson on planning out your homeschool year in my homeschool organization course. Both the link to the video and the lesson can be found in the Resource Section of this book.

Also remember that creating a course of study—and learning to form before fill—will not just benefit you. It will also benefit your kids. They will be able to see exactly what is expected and required of them. They will see what work needs to be done, which gives them a sense of purpose and peace knowing there is an end to the work for the day, month and year.

Our Prayer

Lord, You formed all that is seen and unseen in this world in which we live. Your invisible qualities and eternal power are clearly seen and understood through all that You have made.

Lord, help me as I form and shape my homeschool. May we not fill a single day with something that is not part of Your plan for our homeschool. I want to be deliberate about the activities, curriculum, and programs that I include in our school year. Give me wisdom to know what is best for our family and stop comparing my plans to the plans that others have for their family. In Jesus name, Amen.

Chapter Seven

. . . .

Getting Organized

Kristi

For homeschooling parents, disorganization is one of the most common sources of chaos and the feeling of being overwhelmed. No, you don't have to be a homemaking expert like Martha Stewart or a fixer-upper maven like Joanna Gaines in order to homeschool. But your homeschool will have a better chance at thriving with some basic planning and managing skills.

Getting organized doesn't have to be ominous. With a little help, we'll shed a little light on how we run our schools smoothly, and hopefully you'll feel more confident as you prepare for your homeschool year ahead.

How to Organize Your Homeschool Day

Tricia

During the twenty-four years I've homeschooled my kids, I've also written sixty-eight books. These writing hours are often early in the morning or late at night, and they are fueled by a lot of coffee and a lot of prayer. But the only way I've been able to pursue both my dream of being a novelist and my dream of homeschooling my children is to be organized.

Because I'm a work-at-home and homeschooling mom, I can't spend hours each day grading papers and planning lessons. I have to be realistic with my time. Pre-planned curriculum like Sonlight and Alpha-Omega's Switched on Schoolhouse have worked well for me during some seasons of life. There is a lot I can do, but a curriculum that saves time by doing all of the planning for me— that's a curriculum I can stick to.

I've had to learn to cut out the good things that try to pull me away from the best things. In my book, *Balanced: Finding Center As a Work-At-Home Mom*, I share an activity that could help you prioritize.

How to clear your schedule

First it's important to ask yourself some tough questions, starting with:

- Why are you doing what you do?

- Are you currently volunteering because you didn't want to say no?

- Did you sign up your kids for an activity because everyone else did?

- How would you feel if you didn't have those things on your calendar?

To think about priorities, I want you to start by spending some time going through your schedule. First, write out everything you have going on in a given week or month. After you have your list, rank everything 1–4 according to this grading scale:

- 1 = Things you have to do: feed children, get them dressed, teach and manage the homeschool, work, engage in personal Bible study, spend time in prayer, etc.

- 2 = Things you should do: laundry, cook dinner, bathe your kids, serve others, etc.

- 3 = Things you want to do, things you enjoy doing, and/or things that help you: social media, Bible study groups, exercise, coffee with a friend, your child's favorite sport or activity, etc.

- 4 = Things you're doing to look good or doing out of guilt: volunteering because you couldn't say no, extra extracurricular activities, things that you think will make you a good mom, etc.

Are you ready for what comes next? It will be hard, but it will be worth it. Cut out all the 4s. Then limit the 3s. Realize there will be different seasons in life when you can add in some of those other things, but as a homeschooling mom, something has to give.

After you've achieved some serious cutting, take a moment to appreciate the white space. It feels pretty good, huh?

Once you have cleared some space, it's then time to add in the most important things. Things that ten or twenty years from now you'll be thankful that you accomplished.

Start by picking five to six things you want to fill your calendar with: family dinners, church attendance, quiet time with God, your child's favorite sport or class. Realize that by making wise choices today, you will make the days to come—and the years to come—so much easier! By knowing what to say yes to, you'll be able to decide what to say no to. For example, we choose to make family dinners a priority, which means that our kids haven't been involved in a lot of extracurricular activities. While other parents are shuttling their kids from one activity to the next, we're sitting around the table, enjoy good food and each other's company.

It's not easy to make these types of decisions. The key to success starts with organizing your thoughts. Success means carefully choosing what you won't do as much as it means choosing what you will do. Success means knowing and using your priorities to benefit yourself, your kids, and your homeschooling day. And mostly, success means understanding your homeschooling life won't look like anyone else's—and that's a good thing. More than that... it's a God thing!

How to Organize Your Homeschool Year

Kristi

When I first started homeschooling I searched endlessly for the best way to organize all our homeschool stuff, overflowing, overwhelming STUFF! Now that I've been homeschooling for almost ten years, you can imagine all the stuff I've accumulated through the years.

I'd Google "homeschool organization" and get pretty pictures of very tidy and organized homeschool rooms. That's not what I wanted. I wanted to know how people organized all their textbooks, notebooks, workbooks, worksheets, pencils, papers, rulers, scissors, glue... Phew. The list goes on and on. How did they get set for each day's work? Where did they store it? "Tell me, please!" I'd shout to my computer. I was desperate to figure out how to best set up our homeschool and how to make it run smoothly.

I'd love to say I found the perfect post or site, but there was nothing I found back then to help me. So, I started experimenting. We've tried a lot of different systems. Some worked, some didn't. Many just needed a bit of tweaking to get them to work for us.

Now I have several systems that I use to keep us organized. I've created an entire homeschool organization video course explaining my various systems and how I use them. You can find more information about it in the resource section. I even have a YouTube video that gives an overview of how I organize my school. Again, I'll have that link in the resource section. However, I did want to share my very favorite system with you here: my crate system.

I've shared my crate system with so many people, and pretty much everyone agrees that nothing makes a homeschool run better than this.

My #CloverCrate System

My crate houses all of our homeschool work for the whole year. It's amazing! When we first started homeschooling, I wasted so many mornings racing around trying to get everything together that we needed just so we could start our school day. Now, it's all planned out and in the crate.

Setting up your own crate system is pretty easy. All you have to do is buy a crate designed to hold hanging files, then (obviously) buy some hanging files, and a box of three-tab file folders per child. I color code my kids so we can keep everyone's work easily identifiable. So I suggest getting a different color box of file folders for each child.

Basically, you need one hanging file for each week. In each weekly hanging file you will put a different colored file folder for each child. Each file folder will hold all the child's work for the week.

This is the part that usually scares people. I tear apart almost all of our workbooks! Shocking! I know! I don't care if it's bound. I tear them apart and section them out by the appropriate number for pages for each week. I do this for as many subjects as I can.

This system has truly revolutionized the way our homeschool runs. My older boys are now independent with their work, since they aren't waiting for me to get them their work for the day. They know exactly what they need to do.

What's great is that my kids can work ahead if they want. They just grab their work from the next folder. I find they get really motivated to finish their work faster when they have a visual for the work that is expected of them for the week. If they fall behind, then we just add the extra work to the next week's folder or find time to catch up (or skip it, but more on that later).

At the start of each week, my kids grab their file folders and get to work. Some of my kids need help separating out their weekly work into daily work for the week. I use a binder with pocket pouches labeled Monday through Friday for this. However, I do have kids who stick the whole wad of work in their clipboard and dive in.

Daily vs. Weekly Planning

There are so many homeschool planners on the market right now. Most planners are designed for you to fill in your daily work on a calendar. This is exactly the type of planner I rushed out to get the summer before my first full year of homeschooling. As I already mentioned, I was determined to bring some order to my homeschool. I spent much of the summer meticulously planning out our year. I divided up all the work I wanted to get done by month, then by week, and then by day on my calendar-based planner. Cue the eraser dust.

I was behind by day three. I was erasing and re-writing my plans every day. After a few weeks of trying to get my planner to work, I gave up. All my hard work was for nothing.

Life happens while you're homeschooling. Not to mention that most homeschool moms are overzealous in their plans for the year. I know I am. I learned the hard way that daily planning was just too rigid.

Attempting to plan out my entire year down to the day was pretty presumptuous. I was presuming that nothing would be pop up in our schedule. This left me feeling extremely frustrated when anything messed with my perfectly planned out week. An unexpected illness, a spontaneous field trip or vacation, a surprise visit from family—you name it. Life throws you curve balls all the time. So, I've found that it's really important to plan by week and not by a date book. Let me explain.

I still plan out my whole year during the summer. However, I plan out what we want to get done by week, and I ignore the calendar. Confused yet? Well, I plan for thirty-four weeks of school. Each week has a plan. This is where my crate comes into play. I put all of the work that I want each child to get done for the week in their weekly file folder in the crate. At the start of each week when we pull our file folder for the week out, that's when I break things down by day.

I do have a year-at-a-glance calendar that has my planned dates for each week of school. However, if we have a few curve balls thrown our way, we can just take a week off and pick right back up if we need to without having our whole schedule thrown off. No more hand cramps from excessive erasing and re-writing assignments.

Homeschooling has enough learning curves to overcome as you are starting out. Figuring out what the most efficient way to get things organized doesn't need to be one of them. In the next chapter, we're going to talk about getting you your own homeschool materials to organize. And remember, if this is an area you feel like you need more help in, you can always check out the resource section to find more information about my (Kristi's) homeschool organization course. Just remember, balance is achievable if you choose wisely. As Tricia mentioned earlier in the chapter, prioritizing is key. You can't do it all. However, you can accomplish more than you think if you plan properly and learn to incorporate some of these systems and tips into your school day.

Our Prayer

Lord, I love how You are a God of order. You already see the things in my life that I need to learn to say no to in order to best serve my family. As I learn how to organize and manage my home and homeschool, I ask that You help me to be faithful to remember to save my best yes for what is most important—teaching my children to know and love You.

I know that I'm going to have hard days during my homeschooling career. There will be curve balls that come our way throughout the year. However, I also know that I am laying a firm foundation for my children to learn more about You as they explore Your world around them in all the various disciplines of education. So, help me to figure out the most efficient ways to streamline our homeschool days so that we can take advantage of these years that we have at home together. Thank You, Lord, for Your wisdom and guidance every step of the way. In Jesus' name, Amen.

Chapter Eight

·······················

Homeschool Stuff: Curriculum and Supplies

Tricia

When I think back over my many years of homeschooling joys, I don't think about my favorite curriculum or my to-do lists. I think about my children growing and changing, I think about our family enjoying learning together. My adult kids love to learn, and that's the greatest gift I gave them as a homeschooling mom.

Homeschooling isn't about what you do. It's about traveling the path of learning to love life … and living a life that loves learning! If you do that, you can succeed as a homeschooling parent.

I wasted so much time, money, and mental energy in the past, trying to figure out the right curriculum, I'm here to help you skip those burdensome steps!

Things to Know Before You Buy Your Curriculum

1. Understand there is not one perfect curriculum.

Find something that matches your interest, can be incorporated into your lifestyle, and looks fun to you. As I already mentioned, I've used online curriculum in the past. However, recently I've been using Sonlight. I love Sonlight because it's based on reading lots of books, which I love to do. The teacher's guide gives you a general idea of what activities to do with the books, and my kids love the hands-on approach to learning. It works for us. Look through different options that might work for you, but do not let yourself get stressed or worried over finding the perfect one. Your number-one goal as a homeschool teacher is to guide your children to love learning.

2. Don't compare your children with other children.

I had one child who learned to read at three years old and another child who learned to read at eight years old. Each child will learn at a different pace. Girls will usually learn faster than boys. If you're feeling stressed over your child's abilities, you'll no doubt put stress on him or her, too, which will do no one any good!

3. Pay attention to your child's interests.

Study themes. Does your son love cars? Study engines, design, and the history of transportation. Does your daughter love to bake? Figure out how you can spend time in the kitchen while also learning. Read books about baking, teach measurements, experiment with recipes. I love unit studies for this very reason.

4. Check out free online printables.

This may make me sound old, but the Internet was just putting down its roots when I first started homeschooling. Today there are tons of free online printables. It's never been easier to come up with something fun and creative to do every day. Just Google "free preschool homeschool printables" and have fun! I also like to search on Pinterest.

5. Don't get too stuck in a boxed curriculum.

If you decide to purchase a boxed curriculum that comes with material for each subject, know that you don't have to use it all. Yes, it's hard to stomach when you feel like you already bought a science curriculum with the set. However, if it's not working then look for ways to supplement that subject. You want to look for ways to make learning come to life, so don't get stuck.

6. Don't think of "book work" as a complete education.

Yes, there are great workbooks and textbooks out there. However, when we incorporate real life learning, like volunteering, home economics, and life skills, we offer our kids a more well-rounded education.

Relationship skills are equally important. Instead of socialization, focus on quality friendships. I spent years signing up my kids for community teams and activities so that they could get "socialized." These were often activities my kids didn't care about, and they produced no lasting relationships. Instead, I learned to pick a few like-minded families, with children of similar ages, and chose to connect with them purposefully. Do things together. Share life together. A few lifelong friendships with like-minded families will go a long way.

I can say that I've never regretted homeschooling. I suppose I proved that by starting again when we were almost empty nesters. Don't get stuck or overwhelmed thinking about what curriculum you will use. As Kristi is going to point out, there are ways to simplify what you are going to be teaching. So, don't be afraid to think outside the "boxed" curriculum.

Homeschool "Curriculum" Simplified

Kristi

Picking out curriculum is such a personal thing. Both Tricia and I could rattle off all our favorite curricula that we've used through the years. However, as we've mentioned before, picking curricula based on what worked in someone else's family doesn't often work. One of the best things to do when you are first starting out is to pick what looks like fun to teach. You can (and probably will) change later. That's okay. I did three phonics programs my first year of homeschooling. Now I'm using a fourth. Every child is different and different programs worked better for different children.

One important tip here is not to keep using a curriculum that doesn't work for you or your child! Gift it, trash it, or store it to see if it might work for a different child later. You will save yourself a lot of frustration and tears by moving on to something else.

Probably the biggest misconception is that you have to use curricula to homeschool. You don't. You don't even have to be an "unschooling" family to skip using curricula. In fact, when you are first starting out, it's sometimes a good idea to use a more non-traditional approach to learning while you figure out your homeschooling style and needs.

I'm going to break down non-curriculum ways to homeschool by subject. My hope is that this will encourage you to take a deep breath and enjoy your homeschool experience. You don't have to get bogged down with the stress of picking the perfect curriculum your first year (or so). You don't have to have all your curricula picked out to start. You can take time to explore different curricula.

Reading

Believe it or not, the Bible really is one of the best books to use for a well-rounded homeschool. It's filled with history, science, character lessons, language arts elements, and math. Of course, as Christians, we know that there is so much more than just academic material in the Word. But often we forget just how amazing this Living Book really is.

Exercising your library card, as Tricia will discuss in detail in a bit, is great way to homeschool on a budget. Instead of buying curriculum become familiar with your local library. Pick classic literature to read, like *Swiss Family Robinson, Chronicles of Narnia, Little House on the Prairie, Anne of Green Gables*, and more. Newbery Award winning books are usually really wonderful read-alouds as well. We loved *Carry On, Mr. Bowditch* from these books.

Probably my very favorite books to incorporate into our homeschool are missionary stories. We use YWAM books as well as series like *Hero Tales, Missionary Stories with the Millers*, Tricia's *Prayers That Changed History*, and more. *George Muller* is hands down my favorite biography (so far). *Honey for a Child's Heart* is a resource that has great book lists. I also use Sonlight's booklists as a reference when we are looking for more books to read for a time period or age range.

After we're done reading, I sometimes have my kids draw a picture about what they heard or I have them narrate the story back to me, and that doesn't cost a thing. You can also do a web search for "free homeschool curriculum." The Internet is full of printable resources, videos, and lesson plans that don't cost a penny.

Writing and Penmanship

Writing doesn't have to be overly complicated. I try to incorporate copy work into our homeschool day. Having children write down well-written sentences is an incredible way to have them start learning grammar and writing skills. That's all copy work is. I pull sentences from books we're reading or verses we're memorizing and have them neatly write them out. I also have them write out character qualities from books like *Hero Tales*. Writing can also be as simple as keeping journals, working on creative writing projects, drawing a picture and having your child write a few sentences about it, having them write their own mini book, or having them look at a picture and create a short story or sentence about it.

Writing letters to family, missionaries, sponsored kids, and government officials counts as writing, too. I sometimes have my younger kids dictate a story to me, and I write it down for them. My five-year-old daughter loves to create picture books. She draws a series of pictures and tells me the story for each page.

Spelling and Vocabulary

You can create your own spelling or vocabulary lists from books you're reading or by using a free online program like Spelling City. Those are two simple ways to add spelling and vocabulary to your homeschool. Make it fun by adding tactile activities to your lessons. Having a child spell things out in a pan of corn starch or shaving cream is always a favorite in my house. You can also take a paintbrush outside and paint your spelling words with water on the sidewalk. I try to come up with non-pen-and-paper activities for my younger kids. They tire easily from too much writing. So, spelling is a fun place to mix things up. Actually, this works for almost any subject. We use whiteboards and chalkboards a lot, too.

Math

Math can actually be your tastiest subject. Cooking is an incredible way to teach math. You can teach fractions and counting while you measure ingredients or cut up apple wedges (okay, or pie). There are lots of great ways to learn math facts: flashcards, Flash Master, iPad or computer games, Math Wraps, or board games.

Math is everywhere. Money is a great tool to teach math. And there's always counting. You can count just about anything: coins, beans, noodles, beads, and more! A fun day to celebrate and focus on math all day long is to plan a 100th day of school, just for fun. Again, I suggest including food in on this fun day.

History

History, along with science, is one of my favorite subjects to teach. Your library is brimming with books on all kinds of amazing periods of time and events. Of course, your Bible is fun to use when learning history. Missionary stories are useful to incorporate into your history lessons as well. You can teach your students about the geography of the area or country missionaries are in and even the culture of the people groups the missionaries minister to. Another option is to pick a period of history and study it as a unit study. We have a big history timeline on the wall in our school room. We put main historical events on it and add to it through the years. We have creation, the flood, Jesus's birth and death, family birthdays, and Jesus's return with a date of "???." Just know that you don't have to teach history chronologically for your kids to get the best history education. You can skip around. Just keep a timeline to make sure you don't miss anything.

Notebooking

The Clover kids enjoy notebooking. We create a simple history notebook most years. I have the kids write a few sentences about key events or people we are learning about throughout the year. Sometimes I'll have them draw pictures to illustrate what they are writing about. At the end of the year we have a great keepsake and a nice way to help the kids remember what they've learned. We keep all our notebooking pages for history in order within the kids' binders. This makes it easy to grab at the end of the school year. Some years I have our history notebooks bound, and other years I just put them together myself (hole-punched and tied with yarn).

Science

I love working our way through the creation story. We make our own little creation book that highlights each day of creation. You can spend as much time as you'd like working your way through all these special days of science. One of the easiest ways to teach science is to get outside! God created an entire science classroom for you right outside your door. Start a nature journal and do leaf rubs. You can take nature walks and research what you found, like trees, birds, or animals. You can visit the library and get books about your discoveries, too. Have your kids draw or take a picture of what they find. We've had fun charting the weather here in our city and then comparing it to other areas around the world. On one of our Hawaii vacations several years ago, we melted chocolate with a magnifying glass and studied the power of the sun and how a magnifying glass is convex like the lens in our eye. When we got home we made a big volcano. We've also discovered one of the best science secrets ever: moon phases are best learned with Oreos.

Unit Studies

Unit studies are a great way to start off your homeschool year and have fun. Pick a favorite topic, event, or period of history. Go to the library and get a bunch of books on the subject. Study the people, culture, geography, and science about the subject. Draw pictures about it, write about it, plan field trips, do a craft of some kind, and plan a themed meal. Talk to family and friends who may have special experience or knowledge in your area of study. Take online tours. We studied knights and castles one year. We got tons of great books from the library, built a castle, had sword fights with pool noodles, studied the armor of God, made a castle cake, and had a knight party with a medieval meal. You can even go to Medieval Times or a medieval festival if you have one in your area. We created a fun notebook of all that we learned about and did. There are so many ideas and resources online to help you create your own unit study. Unit studies are a great way to combine subjects.

Field Trips

I always have grand plans for field trips each year. However, I'm horrible at following through and getting us out the door unless we're going with friends. Field trips are one of my favorite parts of homeschooling, but I find I have to be really intentional about getting them scheduled and sticking to that plan. There are so many amazing things to see and learn about first hand from parks, zoos, museums, art galleries, and more. My kids would probably tell you that their favorite field trip was the behind-the-scenes look at a local In 'n Out Burger. It ended with complimentary hamburgers. Yep, many places do that. Don't be afraid to call and find out. I think I need to add Krispy Kreme to my list … or maybe not. Family vacations are great opportunities for educational adventures, too!

Physical Education

I've had so many friends stress out making sure their kids "get P.E." P.E. is physical education. It's moving. So, walk, bike, hike, jump rope, play, swim…just get your kids moving. Of course, different states might have different requirements. Be sure to know what's required in your state. My kids are in competitive basketball, so all of their practice time and games count.

As you can see spending a lot of money when you first start homeschooling isn't necessary. With a little ingenuity you can give your child a great education with very little money. Or, even if you've been homeschooling a while you can switch things up. There is no right or wrong way to homeschool. There is no budget you have to spend. Hopefully we've given you many ideas to have confidence in creating something that is inexpensive yet will work great for your family.

Your Local Library: The Frugal Homeschool Mom's Best Friend

Tricia

Regardless of whether you pick traditional curriculum or take a non-curriculum approach as Kristi just described, your local library is going to be your new BFF (Best Friend Forever!). You'll be amazed at just how many free resources you have available to you at the library.

What do you think of when you hear the phrase, "free library resources?" Just books and DVDs? Today's libraries offer so much more. With an internet-connected computer and a valid library card, thousands of free resources are available to you.

- **INTERLIBRARY LOAN SYSTEM:** Most libraries are connected with an interlibrary loan system, and you are able to check out books from libraries all over the country. Ask your branch about their system. Most of the time you can request books online and they'll find them for you and have them ready for you to pick up when you get there. It's such a time saver.

- **ONLINE DATABASES:** Libraries have a wealth of online resources (databases and e-sources) on their websites for students. What's great about these? They're "referred" sources—

true, authoritative sources far better than Google. Search your library's website for "e-sources" or homework resources.

- **FIELD AND/OR RESOURCE TRIPS:** Plan a field trip to the library with your kids or a group of friends. The children's or youth services librarian will be happy to make your visit so much more than just a tour of the library. One of the things the librarian can do is show your group how to use the online resources available to them. If you're working on a specific unit study or project, she can also gather materials for you and/or help you and the children find materials.

- **BOOK CLUBS FOR CHILDREN:** Many libraries have book clubs for children. I was told by my librarian friend who hosts a weekly children's book group at her library that most of the attendees of her club are homeschool families. Check with your local library to see if they have any book clubs and find out how often they meet. You can even find out what books they are going to be discussing ahead of time.

- **BOOK CLUB KITS:** Some libraries offer book club kits for children. Most kits consist of twelve to fifteen copies of a title with discussion questions if you'd like to do your own book club with other families.

- **PROGRAMS:** Most libraries have monthly school-age programs at the library during the school year. And don't forget the summer reading program! Many libraries have special classes or programs. Look at our local library's schedule. These are some of the things they offer at my library: Family Movie Night, Knitting Circle, Theatre Camp, Writer's Workshop, Snack Attack (Cooking), Finger Knitting, Lego Block Parties, Puppet Shows, and Storytime. I bet you never realized how much fun your library could be.

- **TRAINING PROGRAMS:** Some libraries will schedule computer classes for your children if you ask. There are usually a wide variety of classes available.

- **BOOKLISTS:** Libraries have a variety of booklists of suggested titles for different age groups and on many subjects. This is really handy when you are looking for a particular genre of books to use in your homeschool.

- **HOMEWORK HELP:** Many libraries provide a link to "Homework Help" on their website. Some libraries give you access to websites like Tutor.com for free!

- **LESSON PLANS:** Our local library system provides Arkansas history lesson plans. Some libraries also provide curricula support. Libraries can develop customized booklists, webliographies, and study guides tailored to the unique needs of students. Even if these services aren't available on your library's website, ask a local librarian if he or she can offer this service.

- **ART GALLERIES:** One of our local libraries hosts an art gallery for students.

- **MUSEUM PASSES:** In a partnership with local museums, many libraries provide free passes to local art, history, and children's museums. Warning: These are very popular and are often checked out. Check with your local library to see what's available.

- **COMPUTERS:** In addition to public computers and wireless access, some libraries have laptop checkout. (Check the restrictions.)

- **DIAL-A-STORY:** Our local library has a dial-a-story program. Every day the kids can call a special number and listen to a new story!

- **FREE MEDIA:** Many libraries have a virtual branch where you can download audiobooks to your PC or Mac. You can then transfer this media to your iPad, Nook, or other devices. Our branch also has a virtual reference library with a digital movie catalog, digital music catalog, and digital magazine library. My library uses Hoopla for the digital access, and once I login via my library, it works like a Netflix account. There's an app called Overdrive that also allows you to borrow electronic resources from the library.

- **BOOKS BY MAIL:** Some libraries mail books to patrons free of charge. in some cases, you must have a disability to qualify for these services, but that's not always the case.

Did you know your library could offer all these amazing resources? Believe it or not, some loan out even more than books, like puzzles, museum passes, and toys. You can probably see why your local library could quickly become one of your new best friends.

More Homeschool Stuff ... Supplies!

Kristi

Back-to-school shopping can be so much fun, it's easy to go overboard. We're going to try to create a basic list for some of the essentials for your homeschool.

Shopping list for your school:

- **A BIBLE:** When it comes to reading the Bible in our homeschool, I really like the New Living Translation. It is much easier for kids to understand since it is translated into modern day sentence structures with modern language. I also use Bible apps like Blue Letter Bible, which has great Bible commentaries. The website Bible Gateway is also handy to use when looking for verses on themes or keywords, like peace, joy, contentment, etc.

- **A DICTIONARY AND THESAURUS:** Even though there are apps and spell checkers built into all devices, it's still so important for kids to learn how to use a dictionary and a thesaurus.

- **WHITEBOARDS:** I love having several large whiteboards on the wall (or tucked away that I can pull out) for going over things with the kids. I also have individual whiteboards for my younger kids. Often, writing with a pen and paper gets tedious for little ones, so whiteboards change things up and make it more fun. I occasionally take pictures of their whiteboard work, especially if they've written a little love note. Writing "I love Mom" is the most important copy work to teach your kids.

- **LIBRARY CARDS:** Yep, we are talking about the library again. It really is one of your best resources. I used to get kids their own library cards and let them check out their own books. However, I've found it made returning books more difficult. Now, I mainly just use my card ... and it's very well-worn.

- **WALL MAPS AND A GLOBE:** Another must for every homeschool. I think it's important to have a globe to help kids understand the correct size of countries and context of where places are in relation to one another. We have a large world map for our wall. But I also have placemats for everyone's desk area that has a US map on one side and a world map on the other. I also recently purchased some atlases for historical time periods, so we can see how much countries and borders have changed over the years.

- **A COMPUTER:** I guess I should mention the obvious. We are raising our kids in a digital world. Typing skills are a must. Do use proper safeguards on your devices and keep computers and devices in open areas where everyone can see what's on the screen. There is some seriously dangerous stuff on the web. Be very wise and discerning when it comes to computer use.

- **A PRINTER/COPY MACHINE:** It's really handy to have a printer that has a copy machine function. You can always go to your local office supply store as well.

- **ART SUPPLIES:** Colored pencils, markers, colored paper, glue, glue sticks, watercolor paints, and any other supplies you need for the year.

- **SHEET PROTECTORS AND DRY ERASE PENS:** We love using sheet protectors over worksheets, so we can reuse pages. I also like to use adhesive 8×10 contact paper. It works great for quick laminating.

- **ODDS AND ENDS:** Magnifying glass, educational games, and puzzles.

- **CD/DVD PLAYER:** We love books on tape (and CD). We also enjoy great educational videos. Some curricula requires the use of a DVD player.

- **YOUR CRATE:** Don't forget to get yourself a simple hanging file folder friendly crate and the files and folders to go into it.

- **SHOPPING LIST FOR YOUR STUDENTS:**

- **CLIPBOARDS:** Clipboards make homeschooling on the go easier.

- **PAPER:** Lots of paper. Lined, blank, colored, and construction.

- **PENCILS, PENS, AND COLORED PENCILS:** I give my kids options on what they use to do their work (both with paper and pens). It keeps things interesting.

- **BINDERS OR OTHER ORGANIZATIONAL SUPPLIES:** I also like binder dividers with pouches.

- **INDIVIDUAL WHITEBOARDS:** Great for working out problems together or just giving your kids a fun way to do spelling tests or other work to get a break from pen and paper.

- **THE BASICS:** crayons, scissors, glue sticks, and more.

Most people suffer from paralysis of analysis when it comes to picking curricula and preparing for their homeschool journey. Unlike the generation of homeschool parents before us, our generation has a smorgasbord of choices. Too many choices, it seems. Yet, if you remember our Top 10 Tips in Chapter One, we told you that you didn't have to have everything figured out to get started. You don't need all your curricula picked out for each subject and each child in order to begin.

Our hope in this chapter is for you to see that there is a way to start simply. Take your time discovering what curricula might work best for your family. There's no need to have everything chosen and purchased before your first day of school. You really only need a library card and some creativity!

Our Prayer

Lord, I'm so thankful for all the resources You've provided to me as a homeschooling parent. I'm thankful for all those who've gone before me and have prepared curricula for me to use. I'm thankful for the all free resources available, too.

Help me, Lord, not to get overwhelmed by this great responsibility. Instead, help me to remember that at the end of our homeschooling journey, it won't be about the books or materials we use. Instead our journey will be about growing children who love to learn. It will also be about experiencing life and education together. Help me remember, Lord, that truly successful students are ones who use all the resources given them to impact this world for Your glory. Amen.

Chapter Nine

· ·

Homeschooling the Early Years: Toddlers & Preschool

Kristi

Taking advantage of teachable moments and being intentional about creating learning opportunities is really all homeschooling these early years is all about. The next two chapters are cram-packed with practical tips and ideas to make your homeschool flourish.

Homeschooling Toddlers: The School of Life

Tricia

I'm going to be homeschooling for thirty-five years. That's a long time to be thinking about lesson plans and fun, educational learning. But this second time around with our new kids, I've discovered it's never too early to start homeschooling.

My first time around, I didn't plan on homeschooling. I was a teen mom, and my first son was born when I was just seventeen years old. It was during that pregnancy that I dedicated my life to God and a lot of my priorities changed. God blessed me with an amazing husband and two more great kids (to start). And as our oldest son neared school age, God put it on our hearts to homeschool. I started off unsure but excited. After seeing three kids graduate and go off to college, I'm confident in homeschooling. It's an awesome schooling choice.

Seeing the results I had homeschooling my older children made me excited about experiencing learning again the second time around when we brought home our first adopted daughter, Alyssa. It helped me to realize that it's never too early to start. Here are some ways I started homeschooling Alyssa when she was just two years old.

- **READING:** I started reading to my baby girl as soon as she could hold up her head. Once she was able to hold a book in her hands, she thought they made great teethers, but I was okay with that. In fact, I would often give her a board book that had foamy pages to play with and chew on. As she got older, I would read her a few books a day. Then, something kicked in when she turned fifteen months. Alyssa fell in love with books! Sitting on my lap and listening to a story became one of her favorite things. At least twenty times a day I'd hear, "book, book," and she'd bring one to read. As we read, I'd point out animals, we'd make the sounds, and she'd point out her favorite things. If any page in the book had a "birdie" (which she sometimes called "boppi"), I'd hear about it.

- **COUNTING:** We counted Cheerios on her high chair. We counted toys as we put them away. We counted her socks as I put them on her feet. (That was an easy one.) We counted the "boppies" on a page.

- **LETTERS:** I'm not into teaching my babies to read, but I did buy plastic letters for the fridge. One of Alyssa's favorite games was moving them from the fridge to a cookie sheet, to a tall tumbler, and then back to the fridge. She'd say "D, O, R…"

Even though she didn't get the letters right, she was figuring out that they were letters.

- **SINGING:** Alyssa has always loved to sing. When she was little, she loved to hear me sing! Don't worry about your voice, belt it out, Mama. One evening John and I were driving home from a day trip, and Alyssa was getting fussy. We started singing Sunday-school songs and nursery rhymes. An hour passed without us repeating one song! Alyssa loved it. Now, singing in the car is a tradition.

- **SIGNING:** We first started teaching Alyssa sign language when she was eight months old. We started with three simple words: "more, milk, and all done." We added a few new words every month. (It helps that my oldest daughter, Leslie, minored in sign language in college!) I found some great signing DVDs and books to use when Leslie wasn't around.

- **CHORES:** When she was two years old, I wasn't teaching my baby to do the laundry, but there were a few things we did. She helped me carry items such as napkins, silverware, and sometimes plastic cups, to set the table. She helped me pick up toys. She helped me sweep. I got her a little broom, and she did a great job at messing up the dirt pile I was sweeping up (but that's OK). I wanted her to think chores were fun! (This pays off later, I promise!)

Those are just a few ways I started "homeschooling" my toddlers. I've learned throughout years that the best thing to do when homeschooling is to make learning part of life. I've loved sharing more learning joy with my daughter as she's grown ... and as we've brought home more siblings for her to learn life with.

Homeschooling Preschool: "Sneaky School"

Kristi

I'm constantly being asked what preschool curriculum I use with my littles. It's not uncommon for families to get so excited to start homeschooling that they decide to jump in "full-steam ahead" with preschoolers. Yep, that was me. I already confessed about my homeschool preschool disaster story in the introduction. However, it was not all bad. I learned some valuable lessons that have shaped how I approach homeschooling now.

My answer to this preschool curriculum question usually makes people laugh–I believe in "sneaky school" for my preschoolers. As Tricia just explained, learning is a lifestyle. Regardless of your child's age, the more you incorporate education into your daily routines and activities, the more they will develop a love for learning. I want my littles to have so much fun learning they don't even realize that they're learning. I want to nurture their natural desire to learn and "do school" with us. And guess what? Playing is one of the best ways to learn.

One of my top goals for our homeschool is to instill in my children the desire to be lifelong learners—to have a love for learning! I love trying to find new ways to teach my kids without them knowing they're doing school work. I'm always trying to find new games and activities for my preschoolers that are exciting, fun, and educational.

Cue the choir! I think we need an "Ahhh-ahhh-men!" sung right here. It all sounds so picturesque. Fun learning times with our toddlers. Who doesn't want to play games and make life a little more educational for our families? But we're moms, and we often have a lot of life being thrown at us—all at once.

Homeschooling with little kids can be quite a juggling act, especially if you have older kids you're trying to get work done with.

We'll get into more tips in the next chapter if this is your situation. Whether you're homeschooling one preschooler or homeschooling with multiple ages, it helps to do a little pre-planning and idea gathering to help you pull off educational fun.

I don't know if you're like me, but somewhere along the line, my memory disappeared. I can sit down during calm moments and think of a million fun ideas and things to do with my kids. However, when we're in the hustle and bustle of our day and I'm looking for those great ideas to flood my mind again, they're gone.

Since I'm a list-girl by nature, I started writing all my preschool activity ideas down. I've been adding to my lists through the years. Anytime I hear of good activities for kids or see great ideas online, I put them on this list (or pin them to my preschool idea board on Pinterest). I guess you can say that this list is fifteen-plus years in the making.

Whether they're learning activities or not, finding things for toddlers and preschoolers to do with their hands is great for their development, and it keeps them occupied! Busy little people is the key to getting things done around the house and within your homeschool. Often, hands-on fun is no more than play dough and a few cookie cutters.

I keep a copy of our Preschool Activity List in my main teacher binder. (This list is provided for you in the Resource Section.) I even keep a copy downstairs handy for those days I need a few extra activities. I try to make sure to have the proper supplies on hand as well. When I'm drawing a blank on what else I can give to my littles to do, I turn to my list.

- **LETTER FUN:** We make "edible letters" like letter shaped pancakes and goodies. Even if it's just buying letter cookies from the store, there is nothing more fun than eating and learning. Maybe it's just me, but my kids seem to enjoy it, too. We are going to talk more about involving their senses when teaching. In this case, we use the sense of taste to solidify learning. We also have some fun dot paint stampers that we use to stamp out letters and shapes. Another fun game with letters is to attach a paperclip to pieces of paper with letters written on them. Then just have your kids "fish" for letters with a magnet attached to a string as you call out letter names or sounds.

- **ART FUN:** There are so many fun art books for preschoolers. However, I've found that unless I plan to have all the supplies ready to go, I don't always get to them. So, often I just use what I have around the house. Art activities don't have to be over the top to be fun. Simply getting everyone finger painting, marble painting, and coloring is all it takes to add some "art" to your day. Curious about marble painting? Let me explain. We put paper in the bottom of a cake pan (something with edges). Then we dip our marbles in paint and roll them around in the pan to create some fun designs. Another fun activity is to take cookie cutters and stamp shapes on the carpet.

- **GAMES:** One thing to know about my family is that we are gamers—only not like your modern day gamers. We're old fashioned gamers. We like board games. In fact, one of our "first day of school" traditions is that my kids wake up to a wrapped board game on the counter. Everyone is always excited to see what I've picked. A few of our favorite games for preschoolers are Twister (teaches left vs. right and colors), Pegs in the Park (teaches plus and minus signs), Sequence for Kids (teaches animals and patterns), Candy Land (teaches colors), Cranium's Cariboo (teaches letters, numbers, and shapes), and one of our very favorites, Monopoly Junior (teaches math and capitalism). Ha! Ha! I just threw that one in there to see if you were still paying attention.

- **SCIENCE FUN:** I love science. So, we try to do a few fun science projects from time to time. One activity my kids enjoyed was using sidewalk chalk and creating a human sundial. Building your own volcano is easy with a water bottle, vinegar, baking soda, and dirt. Don't forget to add dinos and army men to make it more fun. Nature journaling is probably the easiest science activity we've done. I have my kids draw what they see, rub leaves, or even take pictures when we're out on walks.

- **AUDIOBOOK FUN:** Audiobooks are also a homeschool mom's best friend. Adventures in Odyssey is always a winner in my house (or car). Jonathan Park is another great audio series of incredible creation-based adventures. It may be for slightly older kids (6+), but I wanted to mention it here, too. Your local library may have some audio books to try out, too. Any audiobook performed by Jim Weiss is sure to be fun.

- **MUSIC FUN:** We are a musical family. We love to sing, dance, and listen to music. I try to keep a playlist on my phone for the kids to listen to during school and CDs handy with some of our favorite songs. One of my personal favorites is Steve Green's Hide 'Em in Your Heart CDs. These CDs are awesome for Scripture memorization!

- **BOOK FUN:** Maybe I should have had this one at the top of my list. Whether it's picture Bibles, board books, or regular 'ol books, reading is the best sneaky school activity there is. Kids love stories and adventures. I try to keep a basket full of books in several of the rooms in our house. Even if my kids are just sitting on the floor looking at the pictures in the books, they are learning. I like creating little reading areas around the house, too. I have bean bags and pint-sized chairs near some of my book baskets. Honestly, if we accomplish nothing more in our day than reading, I consider it a successful day.

- **OUTSIDE FUN AND ACTIVITIES:** Getting your kids outside is important so they can burn off some of that pent up energy kids seem to always be storing. A few of my go-to ideas for fun outside are chalked-out race tracks, yarn spider webs (which is simply letting your kids create their own webs out of yarn), forts, water painting, and anything involving balls. The key is to get them outside and active.

My Preschool Activity List is an accumulation of years of trial and error, as well as ideas I've gleaned from other amazing moms. Just start your own and do a little brainstorming. You'll be happy you did when you're looking for something for your preschooler to do—and be sure to add Tricia's great toddler activities to your list as well.

Teaching preschoolers doesn't have to be formal. The key is to sneak in learning activities throughout your day. Have fun with it. Make yourself a list so you don't forget those great ideas when you've had a sleepless night and need them most. Just let your creative juices flow ... or do a search on Pinterest for ideas. You'll be amazed at just how much little kids can learn at an early age when we don't over complicate things and keep learning fun.

So what if you're facing homeschooling a toddler or preschooler and you have older kids in the house? Well, this next chapter may just be your favorite in the book.

Our Prayer

Lord, we thank You for the precious few years we have with our children as toddlers. The days seem long, but the time sure flies. Help us look to You for inspiration and ideas to make learning about creativity and fun. Bless us with an extra dose of perspective when it comes to the trying times we often encounter with our little ones. May we savor this season of parenting as we look to lay a foundation for a lifelong love of learning. And may we always remember that the most important thing we can teach our little ones about is You. Amen.

Chapter Ten

. . . .

Homeschooling Multiple Kids

Kristi

Whether you're homeschooling one child or a dozen, homeschooling really is about making your way through various stages: toddler years, preschool years, elementary years, and high school years. Often, you're managing multiple stages at the same time, which can feel very much like trying to perform a circus act (there are certainly plenty of clowns and wild beasts in my home). We've loaded this chapter with some really great, practical ideas on how to tame your homeschool no matter how many children (or performers) you have or what stage (or ring) you are in.

Probably one of the hardest obstacles in homeschooling is figuring out how to homeschool your "bigs" when you have "littles." The constant juggling act that has to be performed when there is more than one child in the house can tire out even the most experienced homeschool mom. How do you handle a history lesson with one child, math problems with another, phonics with your pre-reader, tantrums from your toddler, and nurse your baby—all at the same time. Crazy! We'll get into some sanity saving tips like rotating play times for one-on-one time and creating "school time only" bins a little later in this chapter. Homeschooling is not for the faint hearted, but the blessings that come will fill your heart with more joy than you could imagine.

Getting Started When You Have All "Littles"

Tricia

Several years ago, I was asked this question: "My kids are ages four-and-a-half years, two-and-a-half years, and ten-and-a-half months old. I am intimidated to homeschool them for some reason! You've been home-educating for a while now, I would love to glean from your knowledge and experience! Are there any tips or advice that you can offer me as I begin to teach multiple ages?"

When I first started homeschooling, my first three were about the same ages as hers. As I homeschooled my oldest, I let my second oldest sit in. She liked being a part of what we were doing, and she learned to read before she was four because of it. I also put the baby in the high chair and gave him things to play with that he only got to play with during that time. That only worked for so long, but he learned to play at the table (or under the table) while we worked.

Now we're starting all over again with seven adopted children. Over the last several years, I've gotten to re-live those early years. While I'm working on projects with the elementary-aged girls, my son plays with cars (sometimes under the table). He's learning to sit and listen to me read stories, so that's the first step.

Boys are naturally slower at school stuff, so when my older boys were younger, I'd incorporate learning into games. For example, we'd play with cars and count them. We'd play with play dough and learn shapes. We'd read and watch educational DVDs. We'd go on nature walks. We'd memorize things together in the car. (I had some great CDs with states and capitals, etc.) Sitting down and making my boys do work sheets did not work. Instead, I'd pick a topic and focus on that and make it fun.

You don't need to be intimated. Think of it as making learning part of life. Don't worry about finding the right curriculum or finishing books. Get them excited about learning things. The facts will stick in their brains for only so long, but the habit will last a lifetime.

My Biggest Regret and What I Learned

Kristi

Homeschooling school age kids while you have little ones around is one hard task. Our first year of homeschool was such an eye-opening experience. We had taken our two oldest boys out of public school just eight weeks into their kindergarten and first grade years. I had poured so much time and energy into figuring out what curricula to use and how to organize our school room, not to mention how to schedule our days, but the thought of figuring out activities for our toddler to do during this time didn't really occur to me.

I had pictures in my head of him playing happily at our feet while I read aloud to the big boys on the couch. I imagined him sitting at the table with us coloring scribbling contentedly.

About an hour into our first day, I realized this was all just fantasy. I had a toddler who was pulling at papers and demanding our time and attention. You'd think all this would have crossed my mind, since homeschooling with a baby was the very reason I'd chickened out of homeschooling my oldest son when he was entering kindergarten. But our last-minute decision to go for it with homeschooling left me scrambling.

My biggest regret looking back was the number of times I'd say, "Go play quietly somewhere else" or "If you want to be in here with us, you have to be silent." We won't even go into the moments when I lost my patience with him.

I failed to plan! Thus, I, in essence, planned to fail. And fail I did. My poor, sweet toddler was not included in our homeschool. At the time, I viewed him as a deterrent to getting anything productive done.

Luckily, the Lord pressed upon my heart that this was not the way to continue. My busy, active little man had to feel a part of what we were doing, and more than that, I had to make him a part of what we were doing.

So, how do you juggle teaching multiple ages and stages all at the same time? It can be exhausting trying to get everything done, but here are some tips for how we've found success in getting through our homeschool day.

Before we dive into all my practical day-to-day advice on this, there are a few things you need to know. The first is that you aren't going to get everything done. It's just not possible. Even my friends who have one child say that they have a hard time getting everything done. So, you may have to change your expectations when you have littles in your homeschool. It's also important to note that kids between fifteen months to about two-and-a-half years are really the hardest to homeschool with. They are too little to appreciate getting to "play" school with you. Plus, they are too mobile and adventurous to sit still. Remind yourself this is just a season—although my season seemed to be very repetitive.

One other thing to know is that you can relax a bit if your school-age kids are only in kindergarten or first grade.

These grades are all about learning through fun, as we've already discussed. So, have fun! You can get phonics, math, and copy work done in about an hour. Other than that, read, play, and study the exciting things that your kids discover under a rock or in a tree. Take the stress off yourself to do "full-on" homeschooling at these ages. You will stress yourself out trying.

Simplifying is Key

Truly, no matter your homeschool stage or the number of kids you have, simplicity matters! When we first started homeschooling, I bought way too much teacher-intensive curricula. I've since learned to try to find curricula that doesn't require me to teach every element of the material. I also try to combine subjects wherever I can. So, instead of having a separate writing assignment to complete, I'll have my kids write a few sentences about what they learned in science or history. Unit studies, again, are a great way to do this. Don't forget about those awesome audiobooks you can have playing in your homeschool area.

When you have pre-readers in the house, getting as much planning and prepping done in the summer really helps with streamlining your homeschool year. Pre-readers will take up the majority of your time each day, whether it's teaching phonics or changing diapers. In your planning, consider moving some subjects around to different times of the day. We try to plan for subjects that require my help, or that I just want to be a part of, during nap times or after bedtimes.

I heard a great analogy once that homeschooling multiple ages is like riding on a school bus. As you teach your lesson together you let the kids off the bus at different times. So, if you're teaching astronomy, you teach a bit with everyone, but you let your littlest ones off to color a picture of the moon or the sun and learn about the shape of a circle. Then continue teaching the rest of your kids until you let the next child off to work on a worksheet that labels all the planets in our solar system. Then continue teaching your other kids until the next one gets off to write a sentence or two about what he's learned. If you still have kids left to teach, the oldest ones can write a paragraph or even a report about the topic you're studying. This way, you're all learning together, just at various degrees.

Not only do I try to find curricula that will include as many of my kids as possible, I also try to find curricula that fosters independent learning. My goal is to train my kids to become independent learners. Our American history is full of amazing leaders who were self-taught. George Washington, Benjamin Franklin, Abraham Lincoln, and even Ben Carson have inspiring stories about how they learned outside of traditional classrooms. So, don't be afraid to teach your kids to learn independently. I tell my kids I want them to take advantage of homeschooling. It's their education, and I want them to go for it!

Homeschooling with babies in the house

When it comes to homeschooling with babies in the house, naps are key. We try to hold onto nap times as long as possible. I'm very strategic with what I plan to accomplish during nap times. If you're homeschooling with a newborn, I'd first suggest delaying the start of your school year or giving yourself a big break in the middle of your school year to get past some of those sleep-deprived weeks. You need to give yourself an extra dose of grace during the newborn season and stick to the basics—reading, writing, and arithmetic—for your big kids.

Another handy dandy tip when you have babies in the house is to bring all your baby paraphernalia into your school area. Swings, high chairs, bouncy seats, activity blankets, toys—anything and everything should be with you in your room. I even went as far as to install an outdoor swing in the door frame of our school room. Often, I'm pushing the baby as I read aloud. Don't forget there is nothing wrong with wearing your baby in a baby carrier. It frees up your hands, and is the cutest thing you'll ever wear.

Practical Homeschool Strategies for Homeschooling When You Have "Littles" in the House

Buy Them Their Own School Supplies

The first day of school is like Christmas, at least in your toddler's eyes, so don't leave them out. Whether it's just coloring books, crayons, and play dough from your local dollar store, be sure to remember that they want that first day of school experience, too.

Have Bins Filled with Toys that are Only for "School Time"

This summer my daughter got so excited watching me prep our school room with fun things for her to play with. She kept wanting to go in and do school. I'd usher her out and explain that she had to wait for school to start. This just raised her anticipation. Even now that our school year has started, she gets really excited for school time, since she knows that she only gets to play with her special toys and activities during this time. It's also good to note that rotating school-toy bins keeps things fresh and exciting.

Create a Book Corner Just for Them

We love books! We have book baskets in our homeschool. These are baskets filled with library books that are on the subjects that we're covering in history and science. To make my littles feel more at home in our school room, we have two baskets. I fill my littles' basket full of fun books that are either on interesting topics or on similar topics (just at a younger level) as the ones we're studying with my older kids. I keep their books on low shelves, so they can get to them without scaling our bookshelves.

Picture books and encyclopedias are always favorites in our house. I also have a kid-size chair in our school room and a pair of bean bags that seem to float around the house wherever they are needed. Creating an environment that will foster the love of reading is important to me. So when I declare, "Book basket time!" everyone is included in the activity. Of course, having them cuddle up for read-aloud time is always great, too. Another thing to note is that with so many library books in our home, I try to teach them how to care for books.

Start Your School Day with Your Littles

Making sure that you fill their little love tanks at the start of the day will help tremendously! We try to schedule our preschool and kindergarten time for the very start of the day. Some mornings, we walk down to the neighborhood park to get some "P.E." done early. They love it—and they get some energy out (bonus!).

Print Extra Activity Pages for Them

If my bigs are doing a project that has activities pages, I always try to make extras so my littles feel more a part of what we are doing. They feel like big kids, even if they're just treating the worksheets as coloring pages. Allowing them to work alongside everyone helps to instill a love of learning in them.

Hands-on Activities

Finding things for toddlers to do with their hands is great for their development, whether those things are specially designed learning activities or not—and it keeps them busy. Often our hands-on fun is no more than play dough and a few cookie cutters. This is where my Preschool Activity List is helpful. I try to make sure I have the proper supplies on hand. When my mind is drawing a blank on what else I can give to my littles, I turn to my list.

Workboxes

Workboxes are kind of the craze these days in homeschool circles. I've seen them on almost every blog about homeschooling with young kids. When I first heard about them, I was sold. However, they also overwhelmed me as I learned that many families change out their content every day. That just seemed like too much work. So, we use our ten drawer workboxes a bit differently.

For my preschooler, I simply fill her boxes with her favorite activities that she can play with during school time. Her boxes are filled with beads, coloring books and supplies, dot art, pegs, color sorting, and more. My plan is to switch them out as needed, but so far, she's pretty happy with the fun activities inside each bin. She doesn't play with every bin every day. She just picks out what she's in the mood to play with. My kindergartner's boxes are by lesson: calendar, reading, writing, science, spelling, etc. I use her boxes as more of an organizational tool for me, so we don't have work scattered everywhere as we do school. Everything is right where it needs to be.

Create Routine

Truly the best way to get homeschool work done with your big kids is by creating a routine. We have a pretty flexible schedule these days. Our goal is to start school no later than 9 am, which used to coincide with our baby's first nap. We've gotten so used to it that our start time stuck with us.

We also work our day in time blocks. We have things we try to accomplish before we start school, things we try to get done before lunch, and things we try to get done after lunch, during nap time.

Having scheduled nap times is one of the best ways to get work done. I try to have my babies keep their morning naps as long as possible. As I already mentioned, one thing I've learned to do is to move some subjects to our evenings after the littles are in bed.

Sometimes it's easier to do our Bible, history, and read-aloud at night when it's quieter.

One-on-one Time with Older Siblings

I saved my best tip for last. Since we have more than two kids in our home, we're able to rotate "sibling time" into our day. This allows my older kids time to hang out and play with their younger siblings, and it allows me time to work one-on-one with other kids. Sometimes the kids enjoying sibling time just play in a room, sometimes I have an activity planned, and sometimes, I let them play outside. This technique was my saving grace for our homeschool when we first started. We still do it now, though it's changed. My older kids are so independent in their schoolwork that it allows me more time to be with my littler kids.

Although my five-year old is thrilled to be doing school officially this year, she definitely is not happy when her little sister gets into her work. So, we do still have moments when we divide and conquer with the older siblings. This has been such a great relationship builder for my family, too. My oldest actually read Mr. Popper's Penguins to his little brother during their hangout time. It was really sweet.

Homeschooling with multiple children is doable. It's fun. It's crazy. It's life!

Our Prayer

Lord, even though it is challenging at times, I'm thankful for the various ages and stages of my children. I'm also thankful that we can do life together. I pray, Lord, that You will give me patience when it comes to the unique challenges of each age. I also pray that You will show me how to help my children to grow their relationships with each other.

Remind me, Lord, that homeschooling isn't just about getting work done. It's also about growing healthy relationships with others. Help my children's good relationships within our family today be the building blocks that will help them to grow healthy relationships in the future. And may You always be the center of these relationships, Lord. Amen.

Section Two

....

Keep Motivated

Kristi

There aren't a lot of things that I can confidently guarantee in life, but one thing I can guarantee about homeschooling is this: you will have hard days.

There will be days when you feel like dancing around like Julie Andrews on top of a mountain top. Your day will flow beautifully, your children will have "ah-ha" moments, a brilliant, teachable opportunity will pop-up that fits perfectly with what you're trying to get across to your kids. There'll be laughter and smiling, and you'll feel confirmed in your decision to homeschool.

The next day you will wake up full of optimism about the wonderful day ahead and something will happen that will pop your homeschooling-is-awesome bubble. A hard day. You'll have a lot of hard days.

I hate to say this because, for the most part, I'm a Pollyanna-type of person. I'm usually extremely positive and always trying to look on the bright side of life. Believe it or not, my maiden name was Bright. So, maybe I worked hard to live up to my former last name.

But I want to be brutally honest with you. Homeschooling has stretched me. It is so important for you to understand the reality of the frustration and chaos that can plague even the most veteran homeschool mom's life. I can paint you a beautiful picture of all of my favorite homeschool moments through the years, but I also have to tell you the bitter truth—homeschooling will be one of the hardest things you will ever do! However, it will also be one of the most rewarding! (Did you see how I just tried to make that big negative comment have a happy ending? I can't help myself.)

Tricia and I are going to walk you through some of our strategies for overcoming overwhelming days. Our hope is that you won't be blindsided by those not-so-Sound of Music times. You will have really bad days. Expect them! Even my friends who homeschool only one child have bad days. For goodness' sake, I had bad days when my kids were in public school! The Bible tells us that foolishness is bound up in the heart of a child (Prov. 22:15). So when you're parenting, bad days will happen. And so will awesome days! Having a battle plan for hard days ensures you will survive to the end of each school year. Let's get you motivated.

Chapter Eleven

∙∙∙∙∙∙∙∙∙∙∙∙∙∙∙∙∙∙∙∙∙∙∙∙∙

Keeping Your Focus on Your Why

Kristi

No matter how long you've been homeschooling, it's important to remember why you are homeschooling.

About three years ago, I had a girlfriend call me after her first day back to homeschooling and ask me for a little pep-talk. She wanted me to remind her why we were homeschooling our kids. I think my answer kind of threw her off at first. I told her I was going to hang up on her. I went on to explain that I knew why I homeschooled my kids, but she needed to know why she homeschooled her kids. I encouraged her to take some time to remember why she started— and then to write her reasons down.

I can't tell you how important that last part is. It's easy to think about all the reasons you're homeschooling on good days. However, on the I'm going to get a bruise on my head from hitting it against the wall kind of days, you really need to have your whys written down so you can remember them. There's something about knowing why you are doing a task that makes the hard work endurable.

Like I told my sweet friend, I can tell you all about why we choose to homeschool in our family, but you need to know why you choose to homeschool. You'll probably relate to many of the verses and reasons that Tricia and I are about to share. Use these as a starting point to determine your own whys.

Looking to God's Word for Your Why

The first thing I did when we were getting started was to go to God's Word. Anytime I find myself struggling, be it with fear, anxiety, worry, or a myriad of other things, I like to have verses on hand to reference. The Bible is the best resource we have for encouragement, and homeschool encouragement is no different. These verses help me remember some of my why's.

Deuteronomy 6:5-9 says, "Love the Lord your God with all your heart and with all your soul and with all your strength. These commandments that I give you today are to be upon your hearts. Impress them on your children. Talk about them when you sit at home and when you walk along the road, when you lie down and when you get up. Tie them as symbols on your hands and bind them on your foreheads. Write them on the door frames of your houses and on your gates."

For our family, homeschooling is about discipling our kids to love Jesus with all their heart, soul, mind (Matthew 22:37), and strength, and to become lifetime learners through developing a love for learning. Some days, that's all I have to remind myself of to keep going. Other days I have to dig deeper and look at my list. This passage helps me to remember the importance of being purposeful with each moment of my day.

I want to take every opportunity I can to point my kids to Jesus. There is a purpose to education. Whether it's showing them His logic through the logic of math, teaching them to read so they can read His Word, exploring His creation through science, writing out a prayer or psalm, or discovering His hand throughout history. All of the subjects we study serve a purpose when we use them to point our kids to God.

Proverbs 1:7a says, "The fear of the Lord is the beginning of knowledge."

Training my kids to view the world through God's Word is, in my opinion, the cornerstone of their education. I want my kids to have real knowledge, and the Bible says this starts with our relationship with the Lord. In our family, we start there, too.

As Luke 6:39-40 says, "He also told them this parable: 'Can the blind lead the blind? Will they not both fall into a pit? The student is not above the teacher, but everyone who is fully trained will be like their teacher.'"

Not that we are the perfect teachers that we want our kids to be modeling their lives after, but we know and try to point them to the most amazing Teacher who has ever been and will ever be. These verses challenge me to be mindful of the fact that I am modeling through my life and the choices I make.

Combined with the verses in Deuteronomy 6, my husband and I really feel like these passages highlight the importance of parents being the primary teachers and influencers in their children's lives. We also want to be the ones who introduce our kids to other godly people who can pour into their lives. What I found in my experience with both private and public school is that we had no control over the teachers they had each year. With homeschooling, our kids get the same ol' teacher every year ... like it or not.

Fourteen Reasons Why I Homeschool

Tricia

"Why do I homeschool?" It's a question that most homeschool parents ask themselves at some point. Yet since I first started in 1994 the list of reasons why I homeschool has grown as my kids have. I don't homeschool because I want to hide my children away from the world, nor because I don't have any dreams or goals of my own. Just the opposite. I sacrifice a lot to spend this time and effort on my kids. As a successful author with a flourishing career, I could spend a lot more time writing more books if not for homeschooling. I'd have more quiet and more peace. I'd have a cleaner house. I homeschool for many reasons, and here are fourteen that stand out to me:

1. **SOCIALIZATION:** The truth is that sitting in one room with thirty people your own age all day is not reflective of the real world. I want my kids to connect and interact with ethnically diverse people of all ages, as they will throughout their lives. Through homeschooling, my kids interact with siblings, neighbors, kids on community sports teams, and friends of all ages in our ethnically-diverse church. They also spend hours each day with my eighty-seven-year-old grandmother, who lives in our home. This is true socialization.

2. **INFLUENCE:** I want my thoughts, opinions, and values to matter more to my children than those of other kids, teachers, and society. Teachers are wonderful. I love teachers, but many times, their thoughts, values, and opinions aren't those of our family. I want my children to learn godly principles while they're young so they can build a strong foundation for the rest of their lives. The greatest way to teach my children Biblical principles is to model godly living for them, and I'm best able to do this when we spend time together throughout the day instead of a few limited hours at night and on weekends.

3. **FAMILY BONDING:** I want time with my children: learning, playing, laughing, disagreeing, and forgiving. Friends will come and go through life, but our children will have their family forever, and I want these relationships to matter most. My kids need their parents more than they need their peers. They need their siblings more, too.

4. **EDUCATION:** I want to follow my children's unique learning paths, not ones set up by a state office somewhere by someone (as well-meaning as he or she is) who doesn't know my children, their interests, or their talents. I want to choose resources that will provide a well-rounded education with learning methods that will excite my kids.

5. **STEWARDSHIP:** God gave me these children for a limited amount of time on earth. Someday, I will stand before God and be accountable for my choices for them. I take this seriously. I want to be able to tell God that I gave my children (and Him) everything I could when I had the chance.

6. **CONFIDENCE:** We all know that bullying is a huge problem, and I don't want my children to be exposed to harmful or negative words and actions displayed by hurting and negative kids. I want my children to be confident in the people who God created them to be without other kids criticizing them or putting them down. I want their confidence to come from their skills, character, and talents and not because they dress or behave in a way deemed cool or popular according to the trends of the moment.

7. **LEARNING:** I want my children to develop a love and excitement for learning—not just get items completed and marked off a list. I want my child to learn for the joy of learning and not for a standardized test. I want this joy of learning to carry through life!

8. **CONTENT:** I want the material we use to be interesting and engaging, but even more important, I want it to be Christ-honoring and Christ-centered. I want to trust the beliefs and standards behind those who write the material my kids will use.

9. **PREPARATION:** Homeschooling is about so much more than just books. It's about household management, cooking, nature, being creative, exercising our bodies, and serving others. Every day we learn at home and interact in healthy ways, my children are preparing for life.

10. **REAL LIFE EXPERIENCES:** We don't homeschool in a bubble. Our family serves teen moms in the inner city. We visit city parks, museums, libraries, and our city pool on a weekly basis. We meet friends for events and play dates. My children

aren't confined to one room all day; they experience the real life in the real world around them.

11. **FLEXIBILITY:** We can sleep in when we need to or take vacation days when everyone else is in school. We can spend time with dad during his lunch hour (both my husband and I work at home), and show him our school projects as we complete them.

12. **MENTORING:** I'm not foolish enough to think that I can provide everything my child needs. I strive to surround my children with other godly adults (our friends, fellow church members, and fellow volunteers), so my children can see how others serve Christ, too.

13. **HEALTH:** My children spend hours outside each day running and playing. They enjoy healthy meals—all of which are eaten with other family members around the dining room table. They eat far more home-cooked items than fast food or processed food. My children also get plenty of sleep, including naps when they were little, because sleep is important to their development and growth.

14. **FAITH:** I believe in my children's future, and I have faith that God is going to do great things with their lives. This faith causes me to put my needs and desires on the back burner for what I feel is God's greater good for my kids. My faith keeps me going even on days that are hard or exhausting. It's trusting in the good future for my kids that I can't see. And trusting in a God who knew and designed their lives before even one of my children came to be.

Of course, these are reasons why we chose to homeschool, but what about you? Why do you homeschool? What Scriptures guided your decision? What made you consider homeschooling? Take some time and write your reasons down. Not only will this list guide your homeschooling decisions, but it will also be a wonderful resource to look back on during those tough homeschooling days.

Our Prayer

Lord, everything worth doing takes work. It takes perseverance. It takes turning to You to help overcome challenges. Homeschooling is no different.

Lord, during all the times when I feel discouraged, remind me of my true purpose. I pray You will also speak to me through Your Word, guiding my decisions. Ease my heart whenever fear tries to invade, and remind me that if You have guided us to homeschooling, then You will provide daily provision in amazing ways. Thank You, Lord, that You will never leave me or forsake me on my homeschooling journey. Amen.

Chapter Twelve

·······················

Keeping Going When It Gets Overwhelming

Kristi

I literally couldn't catch my breath. I had closed myself in a room and was curled up on the floor sobbing. This was no Hollywood cry. I'm talking blotchy face, runny nose, red eyes. The ugly kind. I was completely defeated. I kept telling myself that motherhood was not supposed to be this hard. I felt alone and beaten. Of course, the moment ended quickly, not because I was over it and felt better, but because my kids found me, and I had to get back to real life— swollen eyes and all.

People don't always see that side of other people's lives. We usually put on our happy faces when we are out and about and post only pictures from the highlights of our day. That's why I think it's so easy to feel like we are the only moms out there who feel completely crushed.

That's just not true. Feeling overwhelmed and alone are very real and normal emotions that seem to accompany motherhood— especially mothers who homeschool. This is why it's so important to reboot our systems and take care of ourselves.

It's Normal to Feel Overwhelmed

Homeschooling: It's part parenting, part schooling, and pure craziness at times. Homeschooling is all-consuming. Homeschoolers are the moms and the teachers. Their job is twenty-four-seven. And maybe that's why we need to ask for help once in a while.

I shared a story in my book, Sanity Savers for Moms, about a time when I was getting pretty desperate for rest and help. Here's what happened:

I remember several years ago having a breaking moment. We were at our homeschool co-op, and I was nursing our fourth little one during the moms' prayer time. We broke up into groups to pray just before we had to go and pick up our kids from their classes. Most of the time I would plaster a smile on my face as if all were well and put my best foot forward. But this time, I was just tired. Too tired to care about what other moms might think.

So, I decided to ask for "prayer." I figured this was a good start. I wasn't asking for help, just for prayer. Well, God blessed me that day. My sweet friend, whom I was sitting with, offered to ask her daughter if she'd be willing to come over and help out. Not only was her daughter saving up for a ballet camp and looking for ways to earn some extra money, but we discovered that they lived three minutes away from me. Amazing! We ended up having this lovely, young lady come once a week for several months to help out.

Words cannot express how much that helped and blessed us. I learned such a valuable lesson that day! Asking for help is sometimes the first step in allowing God to answer our prayer for help. Nobody really expects you to have it all together all the time. No one has mothering or homeschooling mastered.

Ask for help if you're really struggling. The truth is that moms get it, and they're usually happy to help. We've all had hard days—and hard seasons. It's normal. That's why it's so important to make time for rest, and maybe even a little girl time, like a Mom's Night Out.

It's also important to rest. Often we are serving our family all day long—and that's a good thing. For me, this is a gift I'm giving my family. However, I need to get breaks and time for rest and rejuvenation if I want to best serve my family and the people the Lord brings into my life.

Rest will not happen unless we make time for it. We need to schedule rest wherever we can. This could be taking a nap, reading a book, calling an encouraging friend, or just finishing a thought in silence. When is the last time you've allowed space for one of these things? The longer it takes you to try to remember the more likely you need a little rest in your life.

Top Ten Reasons Why Homeschool Moms Need a Break

Tricia

Not that moms need a reason to take a break, but often we forget the importance of why we need one. Here's my top ten list to help you remember to make mom-time a priority.

10. To have a parent/teacher conference—in peace.

9. To dress like an adult again—no yoga pants allowed.

8. To reconnect with friends and talk about things other than curriculum choices and homeschooling challenges.

7. To connect with other moms (from all walks of life) and realize you're not the only one on this challenging parenting journey.

6. To enjoy uninterrupted conversation (unless you count the wait staff as an interruption ... which we don't).

5. To get away from the chattering kids, the multitude of questions, and the squabbling.

4. To finally have a chance to eat without someone stealing your food—or using it as a science project.

3. To fuel up and return happy and rested—a win for everyone.

2. For perspective on life. There is a great big world beyond the kitchen table.

1. To model for your kids what healthy living looks like.

Those are all good reasons, aren't they?

Reason #1 made me stop and pause the most. As homeschooling parents, we know that what we model for our kids is just as important as what we teach. Maybe even more so! If we want our kids to become healthy adults, we need to teach them about learning, serving, giving, caring, working, rest, and recreation.

Mom, if you homeschool, you need a night out. Today, right now, take five minutes to plan when you can have one. It'll help you and your family and will model for your kids what healthy living is all about. Consider it your assignment … and enjoy!

Surviving the Hard Days

Kristi

Exhaustion and hard days happen frequently in our homeschools. In the choice to homeschool, I choose a challenge that still makes me ask myself, "What was I thinking?" at least once a week. All homeschool parents face those days when they ask themselves, "Why did I decide to homeschool? What in the world did I get myself into?" There are days I'd rather climb into bed with some coffee and a good book than figure out another lesson plan. There are even days I'd rather scrub the toilets or clean out my fridge.

I've seen moms throw in the towel and re-enroll their kids in schools. I've known moms who struggle with the nagging thoughts that they're just not cut out for homeschooling their kids. I've witnessed moms curled up in the corner of their room crying out to the Lord to make the day go faster so they can put their kids to bed and get a break—oh wait, that was me.

Like we already discussed, we all have bad days. They are a part of life whether you're homeschooling or not. If you have a child, you'll get overwhelmed at some point. Even if you breath air and have a pulse, you'll get overwhelmed at some point.

Those are the times we're forced to our knees. "Okay, God, can you show up today in a big way? I need you. We need you." And He does show up because, I think, God likes being needed.

I have needed Him a lot, to give me wisdom, patience, and guidance as I train tender hearts and fill young minds. I need Him to guide my days and our school schedule. I need Him to form me into the type of person who would be a good role model for my kids, who are watching me and learning from me twenty-four-seven.

The only way I can teach them at home and survive day-by-day is to allow God to form in me some of that love, joy, and peace that comes from His Spirit. While I don't believe homeschooling is for everyone, I believe that God led me to this choice in order to make me more aware of my moment-by-moment need for Him.

One of my favorite passages of Scripture is the backdrop to the miracle of the feeding of the five thousand. In Mark 6:31-34, we're told that when Jesus and His disciples were tired and needed some rest, they tried to get away by boat, but the crowd followed them. What I love about this story is that it says in verse 34 that "when Jesus landed and saw a large crowd, he had compassion on them..."

Jesus got tired, just like I do. He was the Word made flesh, and in His flesh, He got tired. I'm not alone! I'm inspired by this story because although Jesus had been meeting the needs of thousands of people all day long (and I thought having five kids was demanding), He had compassion and kept working to bless people.

We serve a God who understands those feelings. What I find even more encouraging is that He doesn't tell us we have to go through life using our own strength. Sometimes I think He purposely gives me more than I can handle just so I have to turn to Him faster for strength and endurance.

Getting Practical

Kristi

So when those hard days hit and you feel tired and burned out with your homeschool year, here are a few practical tips to help you survive to homeschool another day.

Pray and Make Sure You're Getting Tme in the Word

This may sound so basic and obvious, but when I honestly look back at my most stressful days, I often find that I was too busy and didn't take time to pray and be in the Word. Now, I try to keep in mind that I'm always going to be too busy, and I have to make time to get in the Word (even if it means putting a video on for the kids to do it).

Get Outside

Whether you plan an impromptu field trip, take a nature walk, or just do school under a tree at the park, break up your daily grind and get outside. I'm a homebody by nature, so this is sometimes hard for me. But the days I do it, everyone comes home happy (and my little ones are ready for a nap).

Slow Down

If you find you're having lots of hard days, it's might be time to slow down. You may be trying to cram too much into your school day. Your kids may need to slow down the pace of a particular subject. There are many things that can contribute to hard days. My best advice is to take a break and do something fun to create some good family bonds. Then once your batteries are charged, start back, but go at a pace that is best for your family.

Get Out those Reasons Why You Homeschool

If you haven't done this yet, you really need to do it now. You will forget. I know we've already dedicated a chapter to this, but there is nothing more empowering than seeing this list on a long, hard day. It will inspire you to stay the course and hang in there when the going gets tough.

Phone a Friend

Creating a support system and getting plugged into a homeschool community are great ways to find the encouragement you need to keep the excitement alive in your homeschool. However, it's really important to know who the right people are in your life! The people in your life who do not support your decision to homeschool are not the ones you want to turn to on hard days.

Calling a fellow homeschool parent is sometimes just the right pick-me-up you need to make it another day. It also always helps to know you're not alone. I've already admitted to being a bit of a homeschool convention junkie. I usually buy several CDs of workshops while I'm there. So, often I find the encouragement I need just from listening to my convention friends while taking a little walk. I get back to the house feeling motivated and refreshed.

Plan Some Extra Fun and Take a Day Off

It's okay to take a day off for fun! Life is educational. Fun can also be educational. We often forget that truth when we're trying to check every box on our curriculum checklist.

Plan something fun to do or mix things up a bit in your normal homeschool day. When I'm having too many days that are causing me or my kids to feel a bit crazy, I plan a "Crazy Day." My kids love it!

When they come downstairs and see me with my clown wig on, they know it's a Crazy Day! We usually go out for breakfast—yep, with the clown wig on—then do something fun like go bowling or play miniature golf. This counts as PE and math, if you have your kids keeping score.

Sometimes we'll just have fun in the backyard with some shaving cream. We have a glass door, so I smear shaving cream all over it and let the kids take turns creating a drawing (see, we're doing art). Sometimes I'll plan a fun little scavenger hunt for our lunch or outing (so they have to read the clues).

We might finish off our Crazy Day with a homemade pizza and popcorn party and watch a fun movie. If I'm feeling really ambitious, I'll have them write a quick, easy sentence or two about what we've done. But most of the time, we just let the pictures we took that day tell the story.

All in all, just hang in there and know you're not alone. Not only did Jesus have tiring days filled with lots of needy people, but there is a whole community of homeschool families out there who understand how you are feeling and who can encourage and inspire you. You may just need to ask.

A Few Tips About Handling Criticism

"I could never homeschool my kids!" I hear that statement almost anytime I tell people that we homeschool. This statement is usually followed up with, "...because I'd kill them" or "they'd kill me" or "they'd kill each other." Apparently, there is a lot of murder involved with homeschooling that I didn't know about.

As funny as these comments strike me, it's not fun when it feels like you're surrounded by critics. It's easier to handle a stranger's criticism than that of a close friend, family member—or spouse.

It's important to mention that you shouldn't homeschool unless you and your spouse are both on board. It's so important to have both parents unified and at peace with the decision. When I started, my husband was a bit leery. However, he did give me his blessing to try it out and see how it went. Now, he's one of the biggest homeschool advocates I know.

For all the other people in your life who like to voice their opinions about your decision to homeschool, let me offer you a few tips:

- **PRAY:** A little prayer goes a long way. You can pray for their hearts and pray for wisdom for how to best to express yourself as you discuss homeschooling with the critics in your life.

- **GET EDUCATED, SO YOU CAN EDUCATE:** Don't misread that! What I mean by this is that the more you learn about homeschooling, the more you'll be able to explain to others about homeschooling. This has nothing to do with how many years you completed in school. The more you read books by, listen to, and seek advice from homeschool veterans, the more educated you'll become on the ins and outs of homeschooling. As you feel more comfortable with the world of homeschooling, you'll find that you feel more confident explaining to others about why you made this educational and lifestyle choice for your family.

- **GET EXCITED:** The more excited you are about what you're doing in your homeschool, the more that excitement will spread. It's really that simple sometimes. I have a friend who's a public school teacher, and she was very skeptical about our decision to homeschool. In my crazy enthusiasm, I brought out all our fun homeschooling books and started showing her all the great things we were going to be studying that year, and she got excited about our homeschool year, too.

- **WHEN ALL ELSE FAILS, USE THIS ONE LINER:** This is the best one liner you'll ever need to respond to naysayers: "I'm giving my children a private, Christian education at a fraction of the cost." I don't know why, but I've found that a person's whole demeanor changes when I tell them this. So, if you are not in the mood to have a lengthy discussion about your choice to homeschool your children with the grocery store clerk, try that.

Just like other things in life, good things come with hard work. Homeschooling will be hard work. However, it will be the most rewarding thing you'll ever do. The time and energy you're pouring into your kids—and the hard days you're enduring—will be worth it in the long haul. I know we may have popped your homeschooling bubble and maybe even forced you to remove your rose-colored glasses. Hopefully, you'll feel encouraged knowing that you're not alone next time you have a bad day. Now you have a few tools to stick in your emergency kit, when you need to refill your tanks move to "Plan D" in your day—a day when your Plans A, B and C fall flat.

Our Prayer

Lord, there are days (weeks, months) I am so weary. I feel as if I have to do it all. I feel as if I can't take a break. I feel as if, no matter how hard I work, I'll always fall short. As if that's not enough, I also worry about what others will think. Help me, Lord, to remember that Your opinion is the one that matters most, and Your strength is what I need to seek most.

Help me to slow down when I need to slow down. Help me to care for myself so I can effectively care for others. Remind me to turn to You, through Your Word and in prayer, whenever I'm discouraged. Fill me with joy and excitement over the opportunity to teach and train my children, and may You be glorified through my efforts, Lord. Amen.

Chapter Thirteen

Nurturing Your Key Relationships

Kristi

Homeschool moms have full plates. We manage a school and a home. Some moms even manage to juggle jobs and ministries. I'm tired just thinking about everything we try to get done in a day. At times it feels like there's not enough time in the day to get it all done. Well, we'll get into the myth of getting it all done in the next chapter. This chapter is about how to keep your priorities straight and to focus on key relationships in your life—relationships that would be easy to neglect because of homeschooling. It's also about remembering to make time for the goals and dreams that God has given you—desires beyond homeschooling.

Keep Your Knees Dirty

We moms are often cleaning up messes. We find ourselves in Cinderella moments, on our hands and knees, scrubbing the floor. Getting our knees dirty is part of the job. However, the most important task we can do each day is to get our spiritual knees dirty praying over our family and our homeschool, and praying for ourselves to get an extra dose of strength.

The first key relationship you need to nurture is the one you have with your Lord and Savior. If you neglect this relationship, the others will never be what they could be. In the previous chapters, we've mentioned spending time in God's Word and prayer, but for homeschool moms, this can be a challenge. How can we make time for seeking God when we have to care for every aspect of our children's lives, including their education? Here's how I've been able to focus on these disciplines in my own life:

- **PLAN AHEAD:** In case you haven't figured this out by now, I'm a planner. I try to make sure that every evening I have my Bible, my journal, any study I'm going through, a pen, a pencil, colored highlighters, and anything else I may use for my quiet time prepared. This helps me to jump in first thing in the morning. Don't forget to have your favorite coffee or tea mug ready to go, too.

- **LEAVE YOUR BIBLE OUT:** I often leave a Bible on a counter or have my Bible app open. Sometimes I just leave my Bible open on my bathroom counter so I can do some reading and praying as I get ready.

- **INDEX SCRIPTURE:** I write out Scriptures on index cards and carry them around so I can meditate on it throughout the day. This also helps me to memorize them.

- **USE SCREEN TIME:** Believe it or not, I have even been known to resort to putting a show on for the kids to watch so I can get a little time in the Word. I try to plan ahead and have good wholesome programs recorded and educational videos on hand. A few of our favorites are Veggie Tales, Owlegories, and What's in the Bible. Audiobooks and audio adventures are great, too.

- **BOOKEND YOUR DAY:** I like to try to start and end my day with Scripture. Sometimes it's nothing more than a Proverb or

Psalm. I keep little devotion books and a Bible on my bedside table.

Don't Forget to Nurture Your Marriage

God, marriage, kids—then homeschool. It's really easy to get these out of order, especially the marriage and kids part. Homeschooling can put a strain on your marriage if you aren't careful. Making time for, and being intentional with, your spouse is so important.

Date nights are a must when you're married, especially if you have kids. You need time away to escape the constant interruptions and distractions. Get a sitter or enlist the help of family or friends to watch the kids so you can get out together as a couple. Be adventurous and try to go to new places, not just the same old standbys. Date nights don't have to be just dinners either. Think of some fun activities you want to try together. We tried taking a dance lesson together on a date night once, and I learned I'm not the dancer I thought I was. We did have a lot of fun, though.

Consider planning a weekend retreat. Again, it doesn't have to be extravagant. We've even had our kids stay with family for a getaway our own home. It was hard to resist getting things done around the house. We had to keep asking ourselves what would we do if we were at a hotel. There may not have been room service, but it was still a lot of fun.

There are times we even have an at-home date night. Mark your calendars, get the kids to bed early, and have some fun at home together. We've done picnic desserts on the family room floor. FamilyLife Ministries has a great kit called "Simply Romantic Nights" that we've used for ideas. Be prepared to blush at a few of them. Focus on the Family also has some fun resources for date nights, like Dr. Greg & Erin Smalley's "Date Night Challenge: Comedy Edition."

Balancing Your Own Goals and Dreams

Tricia

It's easy to think about focusing on relationships with others. It's harder remembering that we also need to nurture our relationships with ourselves. It's very easy to convince yourself that you have to give up all your goals and dreams to homeschool your kids. But by watching you follow your dreams, your kids will learn more about how to follow God and the dreams He lays upon their hearts as they see you do it.

When I first started homeschooling my three kids (ages six, three, and one) in 1995, I thought my life from that moment on would always be about homeschooling. I pictured all of my time (or at least most of it) would be spent shaping my children's education. I scheduled my day in fifteen-minute increments and did my best to stick to it. What I didn't know was that over the years, God would call me to follow my own dreams. What I also didn't realize was that my kids would benefit from my obedience.

It all started when I attended the Mt. Hermon Christian Writer's Conference with a friend. Being with industry professionals made writing for publication seem possible. Classes taught me how to get published. The love, prayers, and support of published authors and editors brought people into my life who believed in me and prodded me to follow God's dreams. It didn't matter to them that I was a young homeschooling mom who hadn't even finished college.

At first I felt guilty for pursuing my dreams. I'd homeschool in the morning, and then in the afternoon, I'd set aside a few hours to write while my children played. Those early years, I wrote articles and ideas for novels as Barney the Dinosaur entertained my kids from the television. Every day, at least a dozen times during those two hours, my kids would ask me for milk, a snack, or for me to play with them. I'd offer what I could but then remind them, "This is Mommy's writing time."

Guilt weighed me down as if Barney the dinosaur were sitting on my shoulders. I was sure I was the worst homeschooling mother there was. To combat my guilt, I swung the other way and became overcommitted, making frequent library trips, signing my daughter up for dance lessons and my boys up for sports. It was my husband who urged me to stop the madness. Over the months to come, we figured out our priorities:

- To provide a godly education for our kids

- To sign up each child for one extracurricular activity a year

- To have dinner as a family

- To train our children how to be part of the family unit and do chores

- To connect and serve in our local church

- To have reading time together as a family at night

- To see what God was doing in our lives and follow Him

For me, this last one included following my writing dreams, and as the years passed, I started getting published—first with articles and later with books. When the kids were eleven, eight and six, God called me to help start a crisis pregnancy center, too, and start mentoring teen moms. During that time, my husband started a dynamic children's ministry at our church. (I talk about how God opened the doors to all these areas in my book Walk It Out: The Radical Result of Living God's Word One Step at a Time.)

With each call from God, I argued. Lord, what about this homeschooling thing? Shouldn't I focus more on that? Yes, I was still spending three to four hours homeschooling every day, but I'd look around and see my friends pouring one-hundred percent of their lives into their kids. I felt I was giving my kids less than I should.

Instead of sitting outside working on nature journals, my kids were with me at the pregnancy center, folding baby clothes or babysitting for the teen moms. Instead of taking those art classes at the museum, my kids were reading or building Lego forts while I worked at my computer. The more success I had in both arenas, the more I felt torn. Yet the more I prayed about the activities, the more I saw God opening doors. Soon I was traveling out of town to research books and attend conferences, and sometimes I had to drag my kids along. (Poor kids!)

> I can't say there was an ah-ha moment, but over time, I began to see how following my dreams benefited my children.

For them, they'd say they realized having a mom who wrote books was cool when we got free tickets and backstage passes to a Newsboys concert through a writing friend. For me, I'd say it was when I saw my daughter's compassion for teenage mothers or when I overheard my son telling someone he wanted to write screenplays. They met WWII veterans I was interviewing and traveled all over the US as I researched.

As a mom, I didn't need to teach my kids that we should follow God's dreams for us and work hard to share His truth with others. They saw that lived out on a daily basis. Being a servant of God was modeled. And here I'd thought I was being a slacker for not doing science projects or having them memorize enough spelling words! As time passed, I realized God asked me to follow my dreams not only for the people I served, but also for my kids.

My biological kids are twenty-eight, twenty-five, and twenty-three now. Cory is married with two children. He has graduated from college and is serving as a children's pastor. He's also a homeschooling dad. Leslie is married and is a missionary in the Czech Republic. She's also a professor at a university there, teaching English. Nathan is writing his second novel and a huge help to me. Still living at home, he's an amazing big brother to our seven adopted children. He's also actively involved in children's ministry with his dad and older brother.

As I mentioned, we've adopted seven kids who are ages six to seventeen, and I can't wait to see what God is going to do in their lives. Even though I have seven kids at home, I plan on doing many things the same, including homeschooling, serving teen moms, and writing … but this time I'm doing it without the guilt. I trust God more now. I trust that if He's called me to something for Him, He understands how it'll impact my kids. I trust He sees their futures, too. I trust homeschooling isn't just about books and learning, it's about serving and following God with everything we have.

What about you? Has God placed a dream in your heart or your spouse's heart? Maybe like me you're thinking, "I'll do that after these homeschooling years have passed." I'd encourage you to go to God in prayer. After all, kids learn far more from our lives than from books. You are your child's teacher … teach them with your life, not just your lesson plan.

Our Prayer

Lord, because homeschooling takes so much time and attention, it's easy to allow other relationships to slip. Help me to focus on my relationship with You first and my relationship with my spouse second. Let me not neglect those who are most important to my heart.

Also, Lord, let me not forget to take time to foster the dreams that You've planted in my heart. They are there for a reason. Since You planted them, You know how they'll benefit me and my kids. Help me trust You in this, Lord. You have a perfect plan for all my relationships. Thank You for all You give and provide to make these relationships strong. Amen.

Chapter Fourteen

······························

Keeping Your Sanity with Homeschooling and Housekeeping

Kristi

As a mom of five, I'm often asked, "How do you get it all done?" Sometimes, I'm struck with the urge to say something sarcastic, like, "Well, Martha Stewart is my mother-in-law" or "It just kind of comes naturally to me." Instead, I usually laugh and confess to the sweet mom asking that I don't.

That's the truth. I don't even try to get it all done. The best juggler in the world couldn't manage to keep all the balls I have in the air. So, my trick is to juggle fewer balls.

You have to pick. You have to choose wisely. You have to set some balls down. You also must simplify your expectations—for yourself, your home, and your homeschool.

Don't get me wrong, I expect great things from my kids, our homeschool, and our household. However, some things have to give. Cleaning, laundry, playdates, field trips, and exercise are all great things. We just can't accomplish everything every day. Pick wisely. Move things around to make things work. Train your kids to help out with housework and meals.

In the season I'm in and with a traveling husband, it's hard to have my quiet time, go for a walk, and shower all before the kids get up every day. (If you can, I don't want to know, because it will just make me jealous.) So, I've found I have to be flexible with my day and give myself grace when I don't get everything done.

Managing Your Expectations for Your House

I don't always get to my housework. My house definitely doesn't stay as clean as it did before I started homeschooling. Of course, I now have five kids. I started our homeschool journey with three. I heard someone say the other day that trying to keep your house clean with kids is like trying to brush your teeth and eat Oreos at the same time. That was a perfect visual.

Last year, when my youngest was two, we would joke that she was our little tornado. She was always looking for adventure, and that usually included climbing up on something and dumping out whatever she could find. I'm sure her little mind keeps thinking over and over, "Will there be treasure in this box? In this drawer? Over here? Over there?"

I've been slowly learning to let it go—not of the house so much as of my desire for perfection. It helps that often, one of my little girls is singing Let It Go!—almost as if to remind me.

Please hear me in that you don't have to completely let your house go when you start homeschooling. There are ways to get things done. (We'll discuss this in a moment.) However, since we are focused on our first priorities, which is God, our spouse, and our kids, know that it's okay to not have a perfectly put together house all the time.

It's okay for your house to look lived in. I find the less I stress about making my house look perfect before friends come over, the more my friends feel relaxed. They can let their kids play and make themselves at home. I joke that my mess is to bless people. I made a YouTube video about keeping it real and showed my homeschool room at the end of the day. It looked like school happened. I've included the link to this video in the resource section of the book.

I don't get it all done, but I do get a lot done. I do get what is most important done. It's a matter of prioritizing and being practical.

Getting Practical

Here are some tips to help you survive the juggling act of homeschooling and housework:

Lower Your Expectations

Something has to give. You may not be able to keep the house as perfectly organized and tidy as you did before you started homeschooling. That's okay. You have to give yourself some grace. Homeschooling is a full-time job. Mommyhood is a full-time job. Just make sure that you warn your spouse that you are lowering your expectations. Talk through the difficulty this is for you and turn to him for encouragement.

Prioritize

Let go of perfection. Just as you make the most time for your priority relationships, you prioritize what is most important to you and your spouse regarding housework. Counters are important to my husband. Floors are important to me. So, we are careful to keep those two things clean and tidy. Know that those are also the two hardest things to keep clean and tidy in our home. But when it happens, usually at the end of the day, it feels so good.

Get Help

If possible, hire a cleaner. This was recommended to me at the first homeschool conference I ever attended by two different speakers. I remember thinking that every woman in the room was probably wishing her husband were sitting next to her so she could elbow him. Truly, if you can find money in your budget to hire a cleaner to come every other week or even once a month for a deep clean, it will be so worth it. I told my cleaners what my budget was and asked them what they could get done for that amount. I thought through what were the most important things that I wanted done, what would help me the most, and I had them do those things. I've been really amazed at how much they can get done on the budget I gave them. Of course, please trust that my house does not stay clean for long, so we still have to do plenty of housework here. But for one hour, the house looks amazing.

Train Your Kids to Help

We are a family, and our kids are part of our family unit. Housework is teamwork. It's not just about Mom running around trying to serve everyone else. Everyone needs to pitch in. Even little kids can be a great help. I start training my kids to help with chores as young as two years old. This doesn't mean that my toddler can vacuum a room by herself, but she can hand her sister the clean spoons from the dishwasher to put away. Teamwork! Most little kids think that chores are fun. Now don't laugh, but I actually train my kids to do the chores I dislike the most: laundry, dishes, and trash. My helpers definitely bless me tremendously, and they don't know just how much.

By taking the time to teach them the most efficient way to do chores, you will also prepare your children for life. Just make sure you don't expect perfection. It takes time to learn these skills. It took me over a year before I turned over the girls' laundry to my older boys. There were so many dresses that couldn't be put in the dryer, and I had a certain way of organizing their clothes. We just kept practicing and tweaking, and eventually they were ready. I tried to encourage them along the way. It's always a great moment when they say, "Okay, Mom. I've got this."

Don't forget to praise your kids for their hard work. I still remember my mom telling me that I was the best sink cleaner and made the sink shine better than she could. I always looked forward to cleaning the sink as a kid. I was so proud of my work. I asked her recently if she did that on purpose to get me to clean the sinks. She told me, "No, you actually were really good at making sinks shine." Her words coaxed the best from me.

Make a List

It's important to figure out what's bothering you the most at that moment. I literally go through the house and write down everything that needs to get done in each room. Pile of papers? Endless piles of laundry? What areas are driving you the nuttiest?

I then focus on getting the most important things done first, and I consider what would be the best plan of attack. I assign each item on my list to myself, the kids, and sometimes, the cleaners.

Of course, some jobs need to be broken down into bite-size pieces. I don't just say, "Clean the family room." We break it down into what specifically needs to get done, then we work together.

Keeping track of what needs to be done and marking each task off is important. I love my white boards! I keep one in the kitchen, so I can write down all the little things I see left out. I can't tell you how much this reduces stress in our home (and in me). Instead of me blowing my top when I see things forgotten or missed, like, as I trip over the shoes I reminded my kiddos a million times to put in their shoe bins, I just add the items to my list! Then I add a child's name or initial next to it.

This helps me remember to follow up, too. I often forget to check on chores in another part of the house when I'm busy getting things done everywhere else. So, this board adds accountability. If you don't have a white board, just use a piece of paper or a sticky note.

I should note that we have an "Extra Chores" list. These are the things like baseboards, grout, windows, etc. that don't always get done. These projects are assigned to the child who needs to have a little extra work. (There's a wink implied with that last part.)

Get Organized

Assign days to get specific chores done. Create a checklist for kids and family—things that need to get done daily. Basically, we try to assign major tasks to certain days and daily tasks to certain times of the day. So, everyone has their own day to do their laundry. Sheets are done on a certain day. Tuesday is Trash and Towels day. This helps me make sure hand towels are actually getting clean on a regular basis.

I also try to meal plan and grocery shop on the same day. However, right now, every child in the house seems to be going through a growth spurt, and I can't seem to keep us adequately supplied with milk, eggs, and bananas. So, sometimes I go more frequently to the grocery store than I like. Keeping to this routine helps to ensure that things get done. Speaking of feeding my growing family ...

Plan Your Meals

Meal planning is my key to keeping everyone fed! Simple meal planning can make a huge difference in your day and save you the headache of trying to decide what to make for dinner every evening. I actually plan out my meals for the week and go shopping one time to gather everything I need. I keep a list where everybody can see it, so when my kids ask me what's for dinner, I direct them to the list.

If you really want to make mealtime easy, make your slow cooker your best friend. I pulled every recipe I could find that was slow-cooker friendly and did searches online for good recipes. I also asked my friends for more. I took this precious compilation of recipes and put them all in one place, on my Easy Meals list, a list that holds all my easy recipes in one place. It is a lifesaver for me.

My Favorite Tools for Easy House Cleaning

Honestly, having the proper tools makes all the difference in housekeeping. I find I'm much more likely to get on top of a mess or get to the daily needs of my house when I have the right tools in the right places. Let me run you through what I use and where I keep them.

- **CORDLESS VACUUM:** I hate lugging out my big vacuum to get to little messes. For the day-to-day jobs I use my cordless vacuum. I keep mine in my kitchen right next to my trash can. Honestly, this is my favorite housekeeping tool! My floors would be very crunchy without it.

- **DISPOSABLE DUSTERS:** I love these handy-dandy dusters. The kids really love these handy-dandy dusters! Dusting is another of my least favorite jobs. These dusters make it quick and easy.

- **QUICK MOP:** That may sound strange, but I mean the mops with the sprayers and the disposable pads. I have a different mop I use for big jobs, but this one is great for quick messes that need more than a little wipe with a paper towel. I keep mine in the pantry next to my big broom, hand broom, and dustpan. I use the wall space to hang all of these.

- **DISINFECTING WIPES:** I keep these wipes under every sink in my house for quick, easy cleanups. This is how I keep my sinks and toilets clean in a house of seven. I also keep a toilet brush and plunger in almost all the bathrooms.

- **BUCKETS WITH BASIC SUPPLIES:** My "bucket list" is different than most. I have a bucket with my basic cleaning supplies under my laundry room sink. Inside it I keep everything my kids need to clean around the house, including all-natural cleaning products, a duster, rubber gloves, rags, and a scrub brush. Having this bucket ready to go makes it easier to get my kids started on a cleaning project.

Housework doesn't have to go out the door when you are homeschooling, only your expectations of being perfect. Know there'll be a season when your kids are grown and out of the house. Your job as a homeschool mom will be done. It's forced retirement! You can focus on keeping things in place then. Then again, it'll still be a good idea to give yourself grace.

Our Prayer

Lord, Your Word tells us that a "wise woman builds her home, but with her own hands the foolish one tears hers down," (Proverbs 14:1). Managing a home and a homeschool is hard work, so please give me Your wisdom. Help me remember that, ultimately, I bless my family as I serve them. Yet also remind me, Lord, that I don't have to do it all or have a perfectly clean and tidy house. Help me to extend grace to myself and my children just as You've offered me grace. Thank you, Lord. Amen.

Chapter Fifteen

....

Letting Go of Your "Super Homeschool Mom" Expectations

Kristi

Often at the start of our homeschool year we have these picture-perfect visions of all we will accomplish the coming months. The amazing field trips we'll take, the gorgeous history notebooks we'll create, the beautiful schedule we spent all summer working on that will get checkmarks as things get completed on time—and don't forget the wonderful time cuddled together on the couch reading from a classic book while the toddlers play quietly at our feet.

Then, Bam! The first week of homeschooling comes, and we are left at the end of the week wondering why we ever thought it was possible to homeschool. It's like Monday morning we're June Cleaver—all skirts and pearls. And by Friday we're Lucille Ball, frazzled hair and furrowed brows, slumped in the corner.

Every homeschool mom experiences this feeling. We all want our kids to succeed and be the best they can be. So we tend to take on more than we can successfully accomplish. I know I get overzealous in my planning, and within a few weeks, I find that we're not getting to all of the things that I had planned. This is normal. We go into our homeschool year thinking that we will accomplish so many amazing things, but we forget that life happens and our kids aren't robots. They get wiggly, unfocused, or stuck.

Busyness, sick kids, sick moms, unexpected guests, curricula that is more time consuming than we thought … You name it and it happens—and we get behind. This was the case for us last year when I had unexpected, major surgery. The recovery was long and hard, and we had to make some adjustments.

Just because you feel behind doesn't mean that you are behind. Often, we feel this way when our kids aren't getting through their work as quickly as we'd like and we start fearing they are falling behind grade level. This is where our advice to stop comparing yourself to public schools comes into play.

Different kids learn at different paces. I see it in my own home. This is the incredible part of homeschooling—we can slow down and reinforce the basics and then move forward again. It doesn't help anyone when you try to push a child beyond what their brains are ready to learn.

This is often the failing point of many homeschool families. The frustration and feelings of failure take over. We won't even talk about all of the unmet expectations that come crashing down. Maybe it's your spouse's expectations or those of a family member, friend, or even the teacher whose class you pulled your kids out of. Often enough, they are your own failed expectations. Wherever they come from, failed expectations—feeling like no matter what you do or how hard you try, you just can't get it all done—can crush your confidence.

This is normal. Most years we fall behind what I have planned for the year. Knowing it's going to happen is sometimes half the battle. What I've found is that there are a few things that I can do to get us back on track again.

When I'm feeling like I'm just not getting everything done that I want to get done, I try to step back and reevaluate what it is that we actually need to get done.

Practical Tips for When You are "Feeling" Behind

Simplify

The first step to getting things done is to pick out what really, truly needs to get done. Do you have to do the pretty history notebook this year and the fancy science lapbook? Maybe you should pick one special project for the year or for a month.

Take Back Your Mornings

I find that if our mornings are off, our whole day is off! I've had to list out all the things we need to get done in the morning and move everything else to other times in the day.

Speaking of your mornings, my advice best advice is to do the worst thing first. This is one of my top ten tips that I give families when I speak about home organization. I've found that it applies as perfectly in our homeschool as it does in our home. There are often subjects that we seem to never get to. When it comes to planning our homeschool, I schedule these things first so I know they'll get done.

Also, there are times I'm just too tired to finish up our homeschooling day when the day has been dragging on. When my little one goes down for an afternoon nap, I'm ready for my break. I don't have the energy or the motivation for the science lab experiment that I have to find supplies for or that art project that I know is going to create another big mess. So, I've also learned to move those things to the mornings when I still have energy for them.

Change Things Up and Make It Fun

Sometimes we just need to shake things up a bit and try something different for a season—or longer. Honestly, the worst thing you can do is to keep pushing a curriculum choice on your child that is not a good fit. Often we get stuck on the thought that we paid for the curriculum that's not working, so might as well finish it up.

Laboring through a difficult curriculum is a greater cost to you and your child. You will spend months banging your head against the wall, and your kids will lose their interest in homeschooling ... or worse, lose their interest in learning!

You may not have to ditch the curriculum. Sometimes, you may just need to take a break from the curriculum and find a fun game that reinforces what you're trying to teach them. Then, maybe try the curriculum again later.

Move Around School Subjects or Combine Them

Combining school subjects is my secret sauce to sanity in my homeschool. When we combine subjects, we can achieve double in less time.

Unit studies are great for this. Remember that a unit study is a teaching technique in which you study a specific subject, like outer space, and then tie all your school subjects into it, such as reading, math, history, and writing.

Don't feel as if you have to buy a unique curriculum for this (although you can find some great ones at UnitStudy.com). You can create your own simple unit study out of any curriculum you are using. Direct your kids to pick great vocabulary words from their history book to add to their writing assignment. Did you notice? That's three subjects in one assignment. Sometimes, a little creativity goes a long way.

Moving school subjects to different times of the day also helps. I found that one year we were never getting to our read-alouds. To fix this, we started doing them at night when we weren't getting constantly interrupted by our littles. We read through many books that way. Just moving the time of our reading made it a success.

Drop Balls

Like I mentioned earlier, homeschool life is a juggling act, and you may have to drop a few balls. You can drop things from your homeschool. It's okay to skip things. Public school teachers skip things all the time. They also rarely finish their textbooks. Do you feel some grace in knowing that? You should. You don't need to cover everything. Math may be hard to skip around in, but for other subjects, you can be selective with what you cover, and you can choose to skip things.

Add a "B" Week

Feeling overwhelmed? Give yourself a break by stepping away from trying to move forward with your lessons. Instead, give yourself time to pause and catch up. We do this all the time. I stop at whatever week we are at, say Week 13, then call it "Week 13B." We spend that week catching up on the key things we need to get done. I prep my "Week B" by picking the things I don't want us to miss out on.

There are some subjects, like grammar, that are harder to double up on. (That takes a lot of concentration.) If we are so far behind that doubling up for a week won't catch us up, then I just skip parts or count on us not finishing the book. Most language arts components are repeated every year. So, if they miss a concept, it's not the end of the world. They'll get again next year. (Just don't skip it next year!)

Fall Behind on Purpose

If you find a topic that you are all enjoying, take some extra time to discover all you can about it. I guarantee your child will learn more in that time of digging deeper than they will if you just move on to the next thing just to stay on track. I love when our homeschool gets hijacked by things my kids find fascinating. It's exciting to see them get excited about learning.

Getting it all done is a myth that we invent in our minds as we peruse the pages of Facebook and Pinterest. Getting it all done feels impossible when we start comparing our messy homeschool day with other people's highlights. You will drive yourself crazy if you try to compare your real life homeschool to the picture you have in your mind of what it should look like. Don't do that. Appreciate your homeschool for what it is. Take time to appreciate each small success. Celebrate what your children learn, and soon your expectations will focus on having fun learning together at just the right pace!

Our Prayer

Lord, we place our homeschool in Your Hands. Help us to discern what the best things are for our homeschool and to relax about the rest. May we remember that we don't have to get everything done just because there is a box to check. Help us to give grace to ourselves and our kids as we go about our days. We want our kids to enjoy learning throughout their lives. So, may we see those opportunities to slow down and dig into subjects that our children are delighting in. We love You, Lord, and we thank You for blessing our homeschool. Amen.

Chapter Sixteen

Keeping It Fun and Creating Lifelong Memories

Kristi

W ho says that only the public-school kids get to have themed days or wear costumes to school? No way! Nothing breathes more life into your homeschool day than planning some fun. I'm a firm believer in intentional fun. We put a lot of pressure on ourselves to give our children great educations, but we also need them to learn the importance of enjoying life.

Fun isn't always spontaneous. Sometimes I have to be very strategic about clearing our calendar enough to allow time for fun.

Also know there are days I'm just too tired to be a fun mom. I'm not very good at coming up with something exciting to do on the spot. Fun will not happen in my home or homeschool without my Family Fun list. When I hear about a new fun field trip or activity another family enjoyed, I write it down. I also create Pinterest boards with ideas for our homeschool.

Fun on Your First Day of School

I have the best memories of my first days of school. I'd get dressed in my new outfit that we'd bought that summer. My mom would often make a special breakfast. I also remember taking pictures out on the front steps of our house just before we'd race off to school. Then, when I'd get to school, the classroom was decorated beautifully and so inviting. Some of the excitement wore off as I got older, though, especially when I knew the homework that I'd be going home with!

First day of school fun doesn't have to be any different in your homeschool than it would be if your kids were in public school. The only difference is that you aren't jumping in the car after you take your first day of school pictures on the front steps—you just head back inside to get started.

Believe it or not, we did a double first day of school two different years. The first time was when I withdrew my kids from public school. We had a first day of homeschool eight weeks into the school year. It was a lot of fun.

The other time we did a double first day of school was when we started back too soon after I had my fourth child. I realized a few days into school year that I was totally useless to my kids because of my exhaustion, so we took two more weeks off and started again. We didn't do all of our first day of school traditions that second time around, but we did enough to make it really fun.

Here are some ideas for creating fun traditions for the first day of school.

Start a New Tradition for This Year-A New Game to Play Together

I have our first day of school present waiting for my kids on the breakfast table when they get up. They aren't allowed to open it until after we finish breakfast. They all know it is a board game, just not which one. The anticipation is fun. They usually start asking what this year's game will be several weeks before school starts.

The rule is that we have to wait to play the game until school is over. This is a great way to cap off their first day of school. It gives them extra motivation to get everything done a bit faster.

I try to find a game that can be enjoyed by the whole family, or at least most members. Some our favorites have been Twister, Candy

Land, Sorry, Monopoly Junior, Mexican Train, Skipbo, Apples to Apples, Guesstures, and Settlers of Catan.

Plan a Special Meal

Whether you make a special breakfast the first day or take them out for ice cream at the end of the week, kids love to celebrate with food. Don't we all! I like to make fun letter-shaped pancakes. You just have to remember to pour it on the griddle backwards, so the "pretty" side of the pancake has the letter printed correctly. Don't make breakfast too complicated, just yummy! The first day can be kind of crazy, so you don't want to go overboard.

Decorate to Add Some Fun to Your Day

The first day of school is a lot like birthdays in our house. I love to decorate the back of each child's chairs with streamers and balloons. I even add a little sign with their name and grade on it. They love it! After the first week or so, once most of the streamers have been pulled off and the balloons either withered or popped, we move the sign to their bedroom doors or their desk area. I usually make their signs using construction paper cut in the shape of a star, but we do switch it up a bit. I try to make my toddlers feel special by decorating their chair with a sign and streamers, too.

Take Lots of Pictures

Like I mentioned before, I have such great memories of sitting on the steps of my front porch for my first-day-of-school pictures. I try to take lots of fun pictures of all we do on our first day. However, when you have littles in your home, sometimes the group picture from the first day of school doesn't always go as planned. We've been known to do "First Day Take Two." We simply take our pictures on another day to recreate our first day. Please take the pressure off yourself if you forgot or didn't find time to get it done before school started. Don't forget to add yourself to the class picture, too. We do try to remember to take last day of school pictures, but I forget most years. It's fun to see how much they grow and change in just a short time.

Have Your Kids Fill Out a "Get to Know Me" Sheet

I like to have the kids fill out a "Get to Know Me" sheet each year. (I have a copy in the resource section.) I have them print their name, grade, age, height, and weight, then ask them questions like what their favorite sport is, what they want to be, goals for themselves this year, what they think their favorite subject will be, their favorite book, and what character quality they will work on this year. For my younger students, I have them trace their names on the sheet, then I play secretary and fill out the rest for them. Part of our last day of school tradition is to fill out a similar form to see how much they've grown and what they learned.

Plan a Special Celebration for the End-of-Summer

We love to have a big campout in the backyard, grill something yummy, and then roast some marshmallows for s'mores for our special End-of-Summer celebration. We usually invite a few friends to come over and join in the fun! One year, all the dads slept outside with the boys. I saw flashlights moving around and heard giggles for hours … from the comfort of my soft, warm bed. We usually try to do our camp out before we start school, but it doesn't always happen. So, we just pick a weekend and call some families and make it happen at some point before it gets too cold to camp. I will admit that when I'm too lazy to get the tent out, we just camp inside.

Buy New School Supplies

I probably don't have to say much about this. Most people get new school supplies before heading back to the books. I really just wanted to remind those of us who homeschool that our kids like to get new supplies, too. We don't have to get everything new again, but new markers, crayons, and notebooks are fun. Again, remember to include your toddler and preschooler in on the fun, new supplies. They look at them as presents, and they want in on the fun.

Start Your School Year Off Slow and Easy

Don't throw every subject into the mix right off the bat. It is overwhelming for our kids (and us) to re-adjust to our new (non-summer) routine. I know our family is pretty relaxed about our summer schedule. So, jumping in and trying to do everything on the first day can leave my kids discouraged and not liking school much. I find starting with a good book to read aloud, some history, penmanship, and math is a great way to start. We slowly add in the other subjects as the days go by. By the third week, we have all of our subjects included into our schedule. Also, if you're using a new curriculum, think about starting just that subject a week before. This helps to get them comfortable with it. Again, go slowly!

Don't Forget Devotions and Prayer

You wouldn't send your kids to school naked, so don't forget to clothe them in the Word and bathe them in prayer before you crack open the books. Even if it's just one Proverb and a quick prayer before your homeschool day gets underway, it counts! We've tried to get our older kids, the readers, into the habit of rising early for a personal devotion. This helps to form a habit that will bless them for eternity, literally. We have a wide variety of devotion books and Bibles that our kids have used through the years.

Write Special Notes to Your Kids

Whether it's on a school desk, a bathroom mirror, or a pillow, a first day of school note will bless your child. Better yet, do this throughout the year. My older boys have Bible study journals they use for morning devotions. I often add a little note of encouragement in there for them to find. Please know that these are not personal journals—they know I look at them. For my non-readers, sometimes I cut out little hearts for them to find. Even simple "I love you" notes are special.

Hopefully you'll find some fun new traditions to add to your routine on the first day of school. Remember, I don't do all this in one day. I spread it out a bit. Just find some way to start your year off on a fun note.

Fun All Year Long:

Don't let the fun end after that first day. Always be aware of opportunities to sneak a little fun into your day.

Fun doesn't have to be extravagant! Sometimes planning an official PJ day and starting the morning with pancakes is all my kids need to think we're doing something really special. Here are a few ideas to get your creative juices going and your fun list started.

Special Meals

This is one of the simplest ways to get your kids excited. Who doesn't love a little food fun? Plan a Color Day and pick food that is only that color. You could plan a rainbow week by picking a different color for each day. Finish up your color week by making some yummy Lucky Charm Treats for the last day as a little rainbow celebration. When we were studying ancient Egypt, I made the boys some "Root Beer Float-acus" drinks as they built miniature pyramids out of foam blocks. We decided that after a long day of working in the hot, Egyptian sun, all the workers would want something refreshing to drink.

- **HISTORY:** Make meals that were popular in that time period. We had soldiers' rations with Johnnycakes when we studied the Civil War. We went to Medieval Times and enjoyed a wonderful medieval meal while watching a jousting tournament when we studied the Middle Ages. Check your library for books that include recipes from whatever you are studying in history. History becomes my children's favorite subject when food is involved.

- **LITERATURE:** What are the characters in your book eating? We're reading Farmer Boy right now, and I'm feeling like it's about time I bought some doughnuts for us to enjoy as we read about all the delicious food they eat at each meal—doughnuts being the food that makes us salivate the most. We ran to the store and bought lemon meringue pie after finishing Amelia Bedelia.

- **GEOGRAPHY:** This almost goes without saying. My kids love studying different countries, since it usually means we get to go out to eat at a new restaurant. Sometimes we try to make new recipes ourselves, but their favorite thing is heading out and getting to eat at a restaurant. We've been to French, Indian, Italian, Japanese, Greek, and Chinese restaurants. We never did make it to the Brazilian steakhouse. That's on my list for next time we study Brazil. You get the point. Make it fun ... and make it yummy.

Themed Days

We love theme days! I'll admit my older kids have probably enjoyed more of my theme days than my younger ones do. This is a little reminder for me to start implementing some of the things on our Family Fun list. Here are a few ideas for theme days for you to try.

- **SCIENCE:** Try a "Water Day," which includes activities like water balloons, a homemade slip and slide, sprinklers, cut-up sponges, and fun pool activities. This would count as PE, too.

- **HISTORY:** "Mini Olympics" are fun to plan when studying ancient Greece. There are lots of fun ideas for things to do with an Olympic theme on Pinterest. Don't forget to wear your togas if you're studying Ancient Rome.

- **GEOLOGY:** Plan an "Archaeology Day." This can be a fun, messy day that includes a dig to discover buried toy dinosaurs using shovels and paintbrushes. Just be sure to end the day with "Dirt Cake." (I'll include a link to my dirt cake recipe in the Resource Section).

- **HOLIDAYS:** Don't forget to plan special, holiday-related activities into your school schedule. I have friends who take the whole month of December off to celebrate Christmas and have special Advent activities.

This list could go on and on. Consider doing a unit study on your favorite part of your lesson—even if you only do that one day of the week. You can be as creative as you'd like to be. Just mix things up a bit.

Spirit Week

Again, who says you have to be in public school to have dress-up days? Plan your own school spirit week. Crazy hair day, twin day, costume day, PJ day—you name it. Just have fun. You can even plan a family party at the end of the week. I've always meant to get T-shirts, hats, or sweatshirts made with our school name on them to wear on field trips. Those would be perfect for a Spirit Week.

Field Trips

Don't stay cooped up in your house. Plan field trips around what you're learning. Explore your area, state, and country. We went to Washington DC last year and learned about American government firsthand. Since we live in California, I plan to do a fun little Gold Rush field trip next time we travel to the Sacramento area. Do a Google search for topics you're learning about and see if there might be some places in your area that coincide with your studies that would be interesting to visit.

Dude and Daughter Dates

This could probably fall into the special meals section. However, I wanted to give it its own special spot in this chapter. It's important to get away and spend one-on-one time with your kids, especially if you have more than one kid. This probably sounds odd, because your first thought is, "Well, I spend all day, every day with my kids. Why do we need more one-on-one time them?" I've found that our days can end up being very focused on getting through our to-do lists if we're not careful.

Spending quality time with your son or daughter is a great way to deepen your relationship outside of your teacher-pupil focused days. Not only do we try to do this throughout the year, I also try to plan it for the beginning and end of the year with each child by planning parent and kid dates. These are fabulous times to get my kiddos alone and get their perspective on what they liked about our school year—what curriculum they liked best, what changes they would make, what they found challenging, etc.

Special Note on Fun

Take pictures. You have to take pictures! Don't be shy about asking strangers to snap a family picture. Nothing makes memories last longer than being able to look back at the photos you took. Making memories is so fun, but the bonus of pictures is that they take you right back to that moment.

Are you already thinking about all the fun things you can do with your kids? We hope so! We hope you have lots of fun ideas and take time to plan fun. Also, remember fun doesn't have to happen by intention only. Spontaneous fun works, too! Every day doesn't have to be a fun day, but every day can have an element of joy and fun.

Our Prayer

Lord, I'm so thankful that You created joy and fun. Help me to remember, Lord, that our school days aren't just about school work. They are also about family togetherness, family bonding, and family fun. I pray that these special times will be ones they never forget. And on days when I'm too tired to have fun, please give me joy. Help me to laugh easily and love deeply. Help me to model a healthy balance between work and play with my kids. In Jesus name, Amen.

Section Three

• •

Bring Out the Best
in Your Kids

Kristi

"Lord, help me not to mess up my children." I find myself praying that prayer from time to time. Some days I pray it regarding my parenting. Other days I direct this prayer toward my homeschool.

Homeschooling parents have so many reasons why we homeschool our kids, most of them center around discipling them in the Lord. In the back of my mind, I still worry about whether they will learn all they need to know to be successful in life. I don't want them to miss out on opportunities because I didn't teach them something they needed to know.

When I start feeling these fears creep in, I remind myself that I need to take a break and pray. These worries are not from the Lord. Most of the time these worries are the lies that the enemy whispers in my ear, those nagging thoughts that creep in when I'm not trusting God for His best for our family. That's what it really boils down to.

I need to remember that God's plans for our lives, our family, and our homeschool are good (Jeremiah 28:11 and Romans 8:28). I need to trust Him with my homeschool just like I do in other areas of my life. His warning not to allow the spirit of fear to take hold applies to our homeschool as well. Did you know that the Bible tells us 365 times not to fear? One time for each day of the year.[1] We read, "For God gave us a spirit not of fear but of power and love and self-control" (2 Timothy 1:7 ESV).

When I sit in prayer and refocus my heart on God's love and His plan for my family, instead of allowing my fears to take hold, I remind myself that God is good. He has good plans for my kids. He has good plans for our homeschool. He will help me to bring out the best in my kids, His kids.

For most families, at the heart of homeschooling is the deep desire to bring out the best in our kids. We want our kids to become men and women of faith who are prepared for all that the Lord has for them. We also want them to have a strong educational foundation. We are going to be sharing some of our thoughts on how to bring out the best in our kids. From focusing on character to giving them a heart to serve, we'll explore different things we can incorporate into our homeschool to allow God's best for our children.

Tricia

Like I've mentioned before, the thing that helps me the most when it comes to homeschooling my seven kids still at home is having already graduated three children from homeschool. I was not a perfect homeschooling mom … not even close. There were times I didn't have the right attitude. There were times I pushed too hard. There were times I slacked off. But through it all, I prayed and I turned to God, allowing Him to speak to my heart.

And you know what I discovered? God is faithful. When I went to Him and asked Him to help me bring out the best in my kids, He did. I love seeing my older kids living and serving Him, and I'm prayerful that all my young kids will do the same. If this is

---

1 Weber, Christian Post Reporter, Katherine. "Rick Warren: Why God Encourages Christians to 'Fear Not' 365 Times in the Bible." The Christian Post. The Christian Post, 30 Apr. 2016. Web. 30 Apr. 2017.

your greatest desire for your kids, too. We hope you'll find this next section helpful.

Chapter Seventeen

Focusing on Character

Kristi

"Focus on character before academics." This is what I heard over and over again from veteran homeschool moms when I first started homeschooling. I knew they were right. However, as our homeschool year dragged on, I found myself just wanting to push my kids through their work to finish the day.

Character Before Academics

It's really easy to get tunnel vision and make finishing the work your goal for each day. Not only are we trying to balance getting school work done—and maybe a load of laundry—we are also trying to balance the right mix of giving our children a great education without sacrificing their character or our relationship with them.

As I've already mentioned, I pretty much narrowed my goals for our homeschool to two things:

Teach my kids to love the Lord with all their hearts, souls, minds, and strength.

Help them develop a lifelong love of learning

When I push too hard and overcommit our schedule with either too much work or too many extracurricular activities, I put these goals at risk. Academics are not as important as the people my kids will become. We don't want to let academics become an idol. In reality, we are training our kids for the most important jobs they will have in life: To be lifelong followers of Jesus and doers of His Word, and to become great spouses and parents. So, even if you study no other subject than Bible, you've had a good day.

Character Starts with Me

Tricia

Not long ago I came across this quote by Max Lucado:

> I choose faithfulness ... today I will keep my promises. My debtors will not regret their trust. My associates will not question my word. My wife will not question my love. And my children will never fear that their father will not come home.[2]

I was challenged to evaluate my own faithfulness. Who do I choose to be faithful to today? Like Lucado, I choose to be faithful to my spouse, my children, my friends, and those I work with. I choose to be faithful to my extended family members, my readers, and my church body.

As a homeschooling mom I can add:

> I choose faithfulness ... today I will keep my promise not to have unrealistic expectations; my children will not regret asking me to read another chapter; my family

---

2 Lucado, Max. When God Whispers Your Name. Dallas: Word Pub., 1994. P. 72

will not catch me stretching the truth or ignoring hard questions; my husband will feel respected, even though I'm busy; and my children will understand that who they are is more important than what they do.

Choosing faithfulness in homeschooling is an action. I choose by making daily decisions and following through, no matter how hard it is. I choose through opening my arms and smiling. I choose by ensuring my thoughts and words are honoring to my Lord and my family. I choose by putting others' needs, especially my children's needs, above my own—and we all know that's really, really hard!

But, the only way I can follow through on these choices is to be faithful and to be filled with Christ. When I take time in the morning to pray, to listen, to worship, and to read God's Word, then I get filled up. Christ's faithfulness fills me and flows out.

If I try really hard, I can be faithful in my homeschooling day ten percent of the time (if I'm lucky). When I fill myself up with God, He works in ways that exhibit faithfulness in all areas of my life—even my homeschooling life. I am blessed as He works, and so are those who are in my little world.

Kristi

Back when I was in high school, I was challenged by my high school discipleship leader to write out a list of character qualities that I wanted in my future husband. She encouraged us to not think about physical attributes that we wanted him to have, so dreamy eyes, chiseled jaw, and golden tan were off the list.

She wanted us to do this exercise because she knew we needed to be focused on what matters most in a marriage. It's so easy to get caught up in the physical qualities and overlook the inner qualities that make a man a keeper.

At some point in college, I realized that as I prayed for God to bring a godly man into my life with the qualities on my list, I first had to exemplify these character qualities in my own life. It was truly challenging.

The same is true in our homeschooling. Before I can expect exceptional character in my kids, I need to look in the mirror. Are the fruits of the Spirit seen in my life and in my home? Am I spending enough time in the Word for His light to radiate through me? I love the way the Bible describes Moses's face after spending time with the Lord (Exodus 34). His face radiated. I want that to be true of me, too.

Homeschooling gives our kids an up-close look at our lives—all day long. Like Tricia was just saying, starting our day in the Word is a great way we can accomplish this. Or, if it works better for you, plan time to read your Bible and pray another time during the day—just as long as you do it. If I want to bring out character in my children's lives, I first have to choose to be faithful myself, to the Lord, to my family, and to my homeschool.

While it's easy to say we need to focus on character before academics, it's hard to do until we remember the end goal of everything we do. Each of us should have these two goals for our homeschool: To teach our kids to love the Lord with all their hearts, souls, minds, and strength, and to help them develop a lifelong love of learning.

In the midst of a busy day, if you only have time to choose one thing to focus on, choose God first. The math sheets and the grammar lessons will be completed on other days, but when we are busy and stressed, that's exactly when we need God the most. It's a true gift to be able to teach our children how much they need God in their lives and how much He can be depended on.

Our Prayer

Lord, it's easy to feel that homeschooling is all about the schoolwork, even when my heart tells me that it's not. Lord, help me to be focused on what's most important. Help me to be faithful in all I do. Mostly, Lord, help me not to fear. I know that fear is not from You. And on days when I'm tempted to require a higher standard for my children than myself, help me to remember that the greatest teaching tool isn't something I buy or teach, but it's my very own life. Help me to live that life well, especially during these homeschooling years. In Jesus name I pray, Amen.

Chapter Eighteen

························

Helping Your Kids Develop a Lifelong Love for Learning

Kristi

We've spent time in the first section talking about different teaching styles and learning styles. Now we are going to break down the easiest way to teach our children, and the most efficient way to help our kids learn. As we will explain, when we combine teaching our children using our unique strengths and interests with teaching our kids in a way that engages their natural bents, and when we do all of that in a multi-sensory fashion, we have the best chance at creating lifelong learners.

Teach from Your Strengths

The absolute best thing you can do to save your sanity while homeschooling is to use your gifts, talents, and strengths when it comes to teaching. Excitement is the best teacher. As Tricia is about to explain, when you get excited about teaching something, your kids are going to get excited, too. So, start with your strengths and watch what God will do with them.

If you aren't strong in some areas, no problem. Find help from a resource or a friend who might have some insight into that area of need. I remember hearing from a homeschool mom who said she had her son call a family friend who was an engineer when they were stuck on a math problem in high school. Their friend was more than happy to sit down over lunch and explain things.

This is actually one big secret of homeschooling. Homeschoolers learn how to learn. When our kids get stuck (and when they stump us), they learn how to figure things out. This sets them up to not just excel beyond our time with them in our homes, but sets them up to be lifelong learners.

Tricia

Let your natural bent guide you as a homeschooling teacher. I love everything literature-based. The curricula that has been most successful throughout the years for my family is based on a lot of reading and writing. I enjoy teaching it, so it makes it enjoyable to my kids. What do you enjoy? How can you use that to benefit your homeschooling? Take a minute to answer those questions.

I'll be the first to admit—I'm the worst math and science teacher on the planet. When my kids did standardized testing, they were far above grade average in everything—except those two subjects. My kids are not math wizards. They have done just enough math in college to get by. Recently, I've hired someone to tutor my older kids in math. I'd rather study ancient history or discuss the themes of great novels than do algebra. I'd rather take a trip to explore historical sites than work on geometry problems, and so I hired someone to do math with my kids.

The good news is my strengths have become my kids' strengths—to the extreme. My kids have excelled in college. My daughter was called out by the dean of her college for her writing skills. My oldest sons are working on novels. As someone who loves researching and travel, we traveled all around the United States, and we've explored Europe as a family. God has multiplied my strengths within my children, and He's using that for His glory. Yes, we might need to pull out a calculator in the grocery store, but we'll weave a great story telling about it!

Maybe you have fears as a homeschooling mom about your weakest subject. All of us do. The great news is that you can turn to God to ease your worries. You can also ask Him to turn your weaknesses into strengths. Over the years, I've come to realize that no child's education will be perfect. The best part of homeschooling is that we did it together, and we've had a tailor-made experience that we'll look back on with joy.

Teach to All Learning Styles

Kristi

There is no greater way for a child to learn than to be taught using as many senses as possible. That's really all learning styles are about: senses. As we already discussed, kinesthetic learners learn best by touching, auditory learners learn best by hearing, and visual learners learn best by seeing. But did you know that best way to retain information and really learn it is by utilizing all the senses? The more senses engaged, the better they'll learn.

Find ways to get your students to move, touch, see, hear, and taste, and then discuss what you are trying to teach them. If you are learning about American history, read great books about people, places, and events from that period. Talk about what you've learned around the dinner table. Listen to music from that era or watch a documentary. Visit a museum or landmark. Act out a famous speech or event. Prepare johnnycakes for the family and ration them out. The list of ways to teach a subject could go on and on. Focus on making learning a fun experience and your whole family will be blessed.

Tricia

It's also important to understand your child's natural bent. Each child is unique. I spent far too much time trying to force my son to sit down and read his lessons and answer questions. I later discovered he was an auditory learner, and it made all the difference. During high school I used DVDs from The Teaching Company. My son loved them and learned a lot, which made me a happy camper.

What I Learned about Homeschooling from the Kibera Slums

I had the opportunity to travel to Kenya with Awana International a few years ago. I knew my heart was going to break seeing the children living in poverty in the slums of Nairobi's Kibera, but I never expected to learn so much about homeschooling from the teachers and students I met.

First, the slums are a hard place to visit. Over one million people live in a community of make-shift shacks, unsafe power lines, and filth. Channels of human waste pool down the middle of muddy pathways, and garbage is mixed in the mud. The stench caused my stomach to lurch.

A pastor friend guided us through the narrow paths, and soon we came to a small courtyard. We stepped inside, and the sound of children's voices met us. Over two hundred children were packed into a small room singing praises to God.

In Kibera most children can't afford school. Many of the children are orphans, and they are completely left to their own devices. They would die from hunger living in these elements, but because of caring people, these children are taken in, fed, clothed, and educated. These schools are not part of the government and receive no funding. Few of these schools have books, yet they have volunteer teachers and caregivers who do all they can to give these children an education.

We guests sat on white plastic chairs as the children gave us a presentation. Because of Awana's training in Kenya, the children quoted Scripture, shared biblical stories, and gave personal testimonies of God's work in their lives. It was amazing!

I walked away thinking of my kids and our homeschool. Here are a few things I recognized:

Passionate Teachers are More Valuable Than Curricula

In the Kibera slums, the teachers had no books or curricula, but they were passionate about teaching. Through Awana training (and the use of a teachers' books and one chalkboard) they taught the children God's Word. The teachers also taught subjects such as English, math, science, and social studies, not because they had the newest and coolest stuff, but because they knew that education would help children achieve a better life outside of the slums. The teachers were excited about learning, not just getting through the lesson plans, and the children were excited, too.

Children Can Achieve More than We Think They Can

In Kibera, the schoolchildren quoted long passages of Scripture from memory. They were able to do so because their teachers worked with them, over and over again. As a teacher, I sometimes give up far too easily. I've found that when I encourage hard work, my children rise to the challenge.

Developing Children's Natural Talents is More Important than Getting the Book Done

In one of the Kibera schools, Beatrice, the teacher, taught jewelry making, dance, and acrobatics. "We try to find the child's natural talents and develop them," Beatrice told me. In a country where the unemployment rate is forty-two percent, Beatrice knows that jobs are scarce, and those who work out of their natural inclinations have a better chance of finding a job and succeeding in life. As homeschoolers in the US, we often look more to the curriculum than to the child. Beatrice's example has stuck with me.

This experience reminded me of the things we've been discussing—our joy and enthusiasm really are the best teachers. Find things you are passionate to teach and start there. You'll begin to see your children get excited about learning as well.

Our Prayer

Lord, You are the Master Teacher. Help us to discern the talents and gifting that You have given to our children and help us to bring out their strengths. Help us also to see the areas that need to be strengthened in both ourselves and in our children. May we bless our family with our passion, and may our excitement for learning be contagious. Remind me, Lord, that it's not about what I buy or have to teach, but it's about what's inside that matters most.

Chapter Nineteen

•••••••••••••••••••••••••

Taking Advantage of Teachable Moments

Tricia

It was an ordinary day. I was leaving the doctor's office with three of my kids when a homeless man approached us. He was in a wheelchair, and he was missing a leg. I'd just gotten the kids buckled into their car seats when he approached asking for food. I happened to have a packed lunch with me. I also had recently been to the bakery, and I'd picked up some donuts for my grandma for a treat.

I gave the man the lunch and offered him the biggest donut. His eyes grew wide. "Is this cream-filled?" It turned out it was, and the man's face filled with joy. He ate it with pleasure.

It was only as I backed away that I realized my kids had been watching everything. Even though I never intended it to be, that was a teachable moment.

On the drive home, we talked about homelessness. We talked about caring for those God brings in our path. We talked about sharing what we had. We talked about kindness. And that night—as the kids shared about the experience with their dad—we talked about it again.

How can you take advantage of the unexpected, teachable moments in life? Here are some ideas from experts (and expert moms).

Converse Creatively

"Learn the art of meandering conversation. When you're working a puzzle with your kids or riding in the car together, talk about worries or other crisis times. As a way to get started, use something you heard about, something you saw on TV, or something that happened to you as a child."

—Ron Rose, *Seven Things Kids Never Forget*

I especially love the idea of sharing stories from my own childhood. There are lessons each of us has learned that can be passed on to our kids.

Be Real

"When I fail, when I say something really stupid, I ask my children's forgiveness."

—Maxine, mother of four children

Being real means owning up to our faults and exhibiting what it means to be humble and thoughtful. Seeing the way we respond will teach our children how to act.

Show You Care

"When uncertainty clouds your children's vision, lead them to their knees in prayer–pray with them often and about everything."

—John William Smith, *Hugs for Mom*

What does this look like in real life? One day on the way to town we saw an accident, and I told my kids we should pray for the drivers. Now every time they see an accident (or even someone pulled over) my children want to pray. Whenever I see concern or worry in their gazes, I know it's time to pray.

Be Available

> "When my children ask me a question, I make a point to stop whatever I am doing to answer it right away. I want them to know I place priority on them and their questions."
>
> —Tamela, mother of two

I've found that eye contact with my children makes a big difference. When I take time to focus on their faces, a connection is made. If they're coming to me I want my children to know I'm available and I care. If I don't take time to listen to my children about the little things, they won't come to me about the big issues of life.

Take Advantage of All Life's Situations

> "I try to share words of wisdom during fun times, like when we're enjoying popcorn and a movie or picking flowers outside. It's then that they're more likely to listen."
>
> —Cindy, mother of five

I can still think back to time when my mom or grandma shared important truths or words of wisdom to me on ordinary days. Those words have stuck with me and have made a lasting impact.

Give Your Time

> "It is clear to me that the time [my children and I] spent together in those formative years strengthened our relationships in their teenage years. Our time together bonded us to each other and laid a foundation of open communication, helping us establish mutual trust and loyalty that grew into a warm, lasting friendship."
>
> —Donna J. Miller, *Growing Little Women*

I've found that bonds are built when I appreciate my children's strengths. Making a list of those strengths, thanking God for them, and praising our children makes a difference in their hearts. And as they grow the connection grows!

Don't Overlook the Teachable Moments God has for You, Mom!

Kristi

Do you ever have those "Ah-ha!" moments when you feel like God just hit you between the eyes with something that now seems so obvious? You know, those "Why didn't I think of that earlier?" times. Well, welcome to my life.

It was almost a decade ago when I first volunteered for this job of educating my kids at home. We pulled them out of public school, bought a bunch of workbooks, loaded up on library books, and jumped in. Full steam ahead.

What has amazed me the most these past several years has not just been how awesome it is to watch my kids learn at home (and to realize how much I never learned in my school years), but to see how much my kids are teaching me.

I'm supposed to be doing the educating, yet there are days when I feel like I'm the one doing the learning. I'm learning that my kids are remarkable at teaching me things I never knew about myself before. They are God's little instruments to teach me the lessons He wants me to learn.

Lesson #1: I am loved even when I mess up.

It's so easy for me to feel unlovable when I think about the bad choices I've made. Guilt steals my joy more than it should. Yet, I've realized that even when my kids make mistakes, it does not diminish my love for them. I love them deeply no matter how perfect or imperfect they are. I've learned that God loves me regardless of my past, present, or future mistakes or poor choices. His love is perfect, even when I'm not!

Ephesians 3:18-19 says:

> And I pray that you, being rooted and established in love, may have power, together with all the saints, to grasp how wide and long and high and deep is the love of Christ, and to know this love that surpasses knowledge—that you may be filled to the measure of all the fullness of God.

Lesson #2: Forgiveness is the key to true joy!

Here's the truth, my kids are awesome, but they are also masters at annoying each other when they want to. I've seen my kids wrong each other. Then I'll watch as the offender will say the obligatory "I'm sorry" to the sibling who was wronged. Next the offended child repeats back the expected "I forgive you" remark. Yet, I've noticed that unless that child actually forgives their offender in their heart and not just with their words, the relationship remains unrepaired and the bitterness grows.

Forgiveness can't be contingent upon whether there is true repentance about what was done or even whether you get an apology at all. Unforgiveness is a poison and allows a root of bitterness to grow. True forgiveness is the repellent to bitterness. It is about letting go of the pain, the hurt, and the feeling of being wronged, and turning to God to experience His peace through releasing it to Him.

If only I had learned this earlier instead of having to see it played out in our home to catch what God has been trying to tell me about the heart of forgiveness. As Colossians 3:13 says, "Bear with each other and forgive whatever grievances you may have against one another. Forgive as the Lord forgave you."

Lesson #3: I don't have it all together—and it's okay.

Not that it took me having kids to realize this, but I feel like it's a daily lesson these days. I used to think that I could handle just about anything thrown at me. I was a great multi-tasker. But I've learned now that I'm not. I have moments when I feel like I'm stuck in slow motion when everything around me is spinning out of control. And you know what I've learned? It's okay! I need to slow down more and soak in the moment. My kids are growing so fast, and I won't get these days back.

So, it's okay to let some things go and give myself loads of grace, because the loads of laundry can wait. As Ecclesiastes 3:1 says, "There is a time for everything, and a season for every activity under heaven."

I'm sure the good Lord would have taught me these lessons eventually. However, He chose to teach me through my time homeschooling my kids.

A God-sized plank hit me square between the eyes: I am God's child! He has allowed me to experience being a parent so that I can learn more about my relationship with Him.

God gave me my kids—my uniquely created kids—to inspire me, refine me, and teach me more about Him and His love for me—His deep, unconditional love. May you not miss the teachable moments that God is using in your life through parenting and homeschooling. Often the lessons that will be taught in your homeschool will be just as much for you to learn as they will be for your children.

When you begin homeschooling, you'll find that life becomes one big teaching opportunity. Take advantage of all the questions that pop-up. Don't be afraid to veer from a lesson plan to delve into something God has allowed to cross your path. Today's teachable moment may just be tomorrow's passion or future opportunity.

Our Prayer

Lord, show me the moments I can use to be fully present with my children. Allow us to take advantage of every second by creatively conversing and experiencing life together. Help me to be sensitive to the moments of life that will have a big impact on my child's life. Help my heart to be open to lessons You are teaching me through my children as well. In Jesus name I pray, Amen.

Chapter Twenty

Giving Kids a Heart to Serve

Tricia

I remember talking to a friend several years back about my daughter Leslie who, at the time, was twenty-one and getting ready to head to the Czech Republic for a year. My daughter was and still is extremely mission-minded.

Since Leslie's teenage years, she's been mindful of reaching out to international people. She's had co-workers from the fast food restaurant where she worked who were from an international work exchange program, and she made quick friends with them. When she went to college, ninety percent of the people she hung out with were internationals. She invited them to our home and church.

Fostering Your Child's Heart for World Missions

My friend asked me what provided my daughter with such a heart for internationals. Here are five ways:

We read through the book *Operation World* during our homeschooling years. We talked about people groups and prayed for them.

We read missionary stories. Lots of them. In fact, when my daughter was ten, she told me she wanted to be a missionary to China.

We served those in our community—those who weren't the same as us. We served at our local pregnancy center, and we served teenage moms. From a young age, my daughter knew there were people—lots of people—who had real needs we could help with.

We went on international mission trips. When my daughter was fifteen, we went on our first international mission trip. In fact, she went to the Czech Republic with her father and me (and our group), and later that same month, she went to Mexico with her youth group.

We hosted an exchange student. Andrea became part of our family for a year, and she came from an atheistic country. She first learned about God in our home. I went to sleep many nights hearing our daughter and our exchange daughter talking ... and most of the time it was about God.

When homeschooling, I never set out to mold my daughter's heart to have a passion for world missions. Instead, I listened to the Holy Spirit's gentle whisper and did the things he asked me to do. Molding often doesn't come with planning. It comes with picking up a book when you feel a stirring within. It comes with saying yes to that mission trip. It comes with opening your home and heart.

Remember that when it comes to your own child's heart for missions, God will do more through your obedience than your planning. Just watch, and wait, and see.

I've seen this from experience. Leslie is now married to a Czech man, and she's still in the Czech Republic in full-time service. She teaches at a university, leads English camps, connects with individuals, and leads a Bible Study in her home.

My two oldest sons are mission-minded in different ways, closer to home. Cory is a homeschooling dad and children's pastor. Nathan is also a writer, and he's been a wonderful godly influence on his adopted brothers and sisters. It's wonderful to see my children's hearts for serving others grow and expand over the years, and I can't wait to see how God is going to continue to use my other children, too.

Five Ways to Encourage Your Kids to Volunteer

You're probably familiar with the verse, "It is better to give than receive" (Acts 20:35). For many families, the best gifts they can give is the gift of themselves ... through volunteering.

Family volunteering has been an interest to homeschooling advocates for years. When I first started teaching my kids, homeschooling pioneers Raymond and Dorothy Moore recommended an hour a day of home or community service. Can you imagine how your family (homeschooling or not) could impact the community by volunteering an hour a day? Even an hour a week would add up in the long run! Here's how to start:

Fit the Activity to the Child

Expose your children to various volunteering opportunities then ask them, "What would you like to do?" Give them resources, then empower them to do it. If your daughter has a lot of energy, or your son enjoys cooking, suggest an activity to match, like mowing a neighbor's lawn or making cookies for the family next door.

Work as a Team

"Through volunteer work, families spend quality time together, help others, have fun, communicate, and develop family self-esteem," says Lori Goudreau, manager of the Family Service Program. "Parents can reinforce family values, and kids can share their time and talents, and even acquire new skills." A lot of what your kids can learn to do will take instruction time from you. All of that is time well spent together.

"Kids are more likely to stick with an avenue of service if they volunteer beside a parent or grandparent," a friend of mine reminded me. Volunteering within the context of their family gives kids the security they need to reach out to others.

Be Prepared

When preparing for a volunteer activity, it's important to know what to expect. Here are some questions to ask:

- Where do we need to go?

- When do we need to be there?

- Who will we report to?

- What are we expected to bring?

- Why is our role important?

Knowing what to expect ahead of time will help children approach their tasks with confidence.

Give Feedback

Kids love to know when they've done a good job. After volunteering, talk to your child about the experience. Let her know how it makes you feel to see her acting in such a mature and giving nature. Your encouragement may be just the thing that will make your child want to do it again. And even if your child is nervous or sulks, even if your child hides or asks to leave, applaud his or her willingness to try. Some kids will enjoy every moment, and other kids might need time to mature. Or they might need to try a different volunteer activity.

Value the Lessons They Learn

I've discovered with my own kids that volunteering helped them establish their identity. When my daughter Leslie was ten years old, she used to babysit at our local crisis pregnancy center. In return, she discovered that her caring attitude and helping heart were valuable to many young moms in need. It's a discovery that has impacted her as she's grown into a young adult.

"Beyond citizenship, kids can learn so many other life-lessons from charity," says Kathy Saulitis, director of Kids Care, a national volunteer organization designed specifically for children. "They learn cooperation, tolerance, problem-solving, communication, self-awareness, confidence, respect for life, and loyalty."

And what mom doesn't want that for her kids? The same spirit that inspired the creation of the Peace Corps on a national level can be a very real part of the lives of you and your children. It may be on a smaller scale, but it can still be a blessing within your neighborhood, which will be just as important a contribution.

Serving others may not come as part of your purchased curriculum, yet the lessons children learn when they volunteer are some of the most important ones. Children learn selflessness, compassion, hard-work, and dedication when they take time to give and serve. Some children, like Leslie, will grow and travel the world sharing God's good news. Others may serve closer to home, but when serving others becomes a natural outpouring, everything in your child's life will change. They will look around and not see what they can get, but instead what they can give. And these are the type of people who will truly make a difference in the world.

Our Prayer

Lord, help us not to underestimate the influence we can make for Your kingdom through living, serving, and learning together. Help us to step out in faith and not allow fear or busyness to interfere with our family taking time to serve on a local or worldwide level. Give us eyes to see opportunities to give our time and resources to bless others. May all the members of our family be more excited about what we can give than what we can get. May each of us grow more like You in this way each day. In Jesus name we pray, Amen.

Chapter Twenty-One

· ·

Growing Godly Disciples

Tricia

Prayer is probably the most important thing you can do for your homeschool. The best thing about starting over again through our seven adoptions is realizing where to place my priorities. Looking back, I now see that all the little things that I stressed about (not coloring in the lines, not knowing multiplication tables by third grade, and not being able to diagram sentences in junior high) didn't matter nearly as much as I thought they did. Instead, it was the little things: the snatches of conversation about God, the missionary stories we read together, and the tenderness I showed them and their father throughout the day that played a bigger part in who my older children have turned out to be.

The Power of Prayer in Your Homeschool

It's not that the minute educational details don't matter. It's just that the spiritual brush strokes throughout the day mattered so much more. As I look back at all my homeschooling years, I can't help but think about Genesis 28:13, "Surely God was in this place and I did not perceive it." Jacob discovered God when he was alone on a mountain, running in fear. I discovered God during overwhelmingly busy school days.

So many prayers have gone through my mind as we've homeschooled through the years. I wanted to share some with you that I hope will be a blessing to you and your family. Use them, trust in God, and repeat!

> Lord, open my spiritual eyes so that I can see You in hectic, busy homeschool days.

> Show me ordinary miracles, and help me to see that You show up when we invite You in.

> Give me patience for wiggly worms, cranky attitudes, and persistent dawdlers. Help me to remember that a love of learning is more important than a worksheet completed neatly and in a timely manner.

> Lord, help me to seek first Your kingdom in our homeschool. Let my eyes be fixed on what's eternal, rather than what's fleeting.

> Dear Jesus, show me how You designed my children, with their unique gifts and talents. Guide me in ways to build on those strengths instead of trying to fit my children into a curriculum's mold.

> Unite our family on this homeschooling journey. May our time together build bonds that will last a lifetime.

> Open my eyes to the books and resources that will help to expand our knowledge of You and Your world.

> Dear Jesus, bring homeschooling friends into our lives who we can bless and who can be a blessing to our family.

> Help me guide my children in physical wellness and healthy living. I know that focusing on knowledge is not enough. Help us to build healthy bodies, too.

Lord, may my first response during tense or overwhelming days be to turn to You in prayer, realizing that I don't have to face the day alone.

Help us to face disappointments well, for I know that character is built when we deal with things that go wrong even more than when they go right.

Dear Jesus, bless our finances. Show us ways to do more with less, so that we can be faithful examples to our children.

Lord, let me not be overwhelmed with all the daily tasks. Fill my heart with joy as I clean, cook, and serve.

Help me, Jesus, to set safe boundaries for my children. Show me how to shelter them when I need to, but also teach them how to deal with the world's struggles while they are still safe in my care.

Help me to smile more than I frown and offer encouragement more than I complain. No one is perfect, but may Your Spirit in me change my attitude for the better.

Finally, Lord, remind me that the prayers that always go unanswered are the ones I never pray. Help me to turn to You first and often. Amen.

Take time to go through these prayers and consider your family as you do. You can use these as a starter for your own longer prayers or journal entries, too. Look up Scripture verses to go with each of these prayers, and soon you'll find your attitude toward your homeschool changing from the inside out.

The Importance of Family Devotions and Apologetics

Kristi

We love reading great devotional books together as a family at night. I'm always on the lookout for good books that we can go through with our kids for our evening devotions. We have a variety of Bibles that we go through with our kids at various ages. We have beginner Bibles for the little ones, then story Bibles for our not-so-little ones. However, we also like to mix in great devotional books from time-to-time.

We've had many favorites through the years, namely books by Bob Schultz. His *Created for Work* book was recommended to me by a fellow homeschool mom as a good book to read aloud with boys. The chapters were so good and meaty and filled with wonderful nuggets of wisdom from a man who poured out the lessons God had taught him through the years onto the pages of his books.

Missionary stories are another family favorite. We sometimes incorporate these books into our homeschool day. However, they also make great family devotion books. Missionary stories show our kids real life ways that God has shown up—sometimes in miraculous ways!

What my husband and I have found is that no matter what book we're reading together, it's important to take time to share our own impression of what we read and to ask questions. Helping our kids to dissect the Bible or whatever faith-based book we are going through is a lesson in and of itself. I do love it when books have questions at the end of a chapter, so I don't have to come up with my own, but it's not that hard to come up with a few questions when we finish our time reading together.

We try to ask questions about the person we are reading about or the theme or lesson of the chapter. Sometimes, we stick to basic questions: Who is it about? When is it happening? Where is it set?

What is the theme? One question we always try to ask is, "How does this apply to us?" or "What can we learn from this?"

After we've asked our questions and had a conversation about the book, we share our perspective. This helps our kids see how to read through a book and gain wisdom and insight. Basically, we are training our kids how to learn from their time in the Word and their time reading great books from men and women of faith.

Books on apologetics are equally important to include in our home. I honestly believe that the culture of the world we live in requires us to be training up our children in a manner that prepares them to defend their faith—whether they are homeschooled or not. That's really what apologetics is: learning how to communicate our faith and the reason for our faith.

As 1 Peter 3:15 says, "Always be prepared to give an answer to everyone who asks you to give a reason for the hope that you have. But do this with gentleness and respect." So, many of the books we choose for our family devotions have elements of apologetics in them. Sometimes, we have discussions on how to answer people when they ask us questions about our faith. We'll include a few of our favorite books on apologetics in the resource sections.

As much as we want our children to gain an exceptional education while they're at home with us, our ultimate goal is to train them to love and serve the Lord. Praying over our family and our homeschool is so important. However, don't forget about discipling your kids along the way as well. Teaching them how to pray, read the Bible, and figure out how God's Word applies to their lives will be one of the most important life lessons they might ever learn under your roof.

Our Prayer

Lord, help us to treasure this time that we have our children at home with us. May we be purposeful in our training of them so that "when they are old they will not turn from it" (Proverbs 22:6). We desire for our children to walk in Your truth all the days of their lives. There would be no greater joy for us as parents (2 John 1:4). Grant us Your diligence and steadfastness to make discipling our children one of the top priorities in our homeschool. In Jesus name we pray, Amen.

Chapter Twenty-Two

Homeschooling Children with Learning Difficulties or a Strong Will

Tricia

From the first moment we discover we're pregnant, we have dreams for our child. Dreams of who they will be and what they will accomplish. We marvel at first words and cheer on first sentences. We imagine story times and science projects to come.

Yet when a child has learning difficulties, we are often discouraged and disappointed. We may wonder if we did something wrong. Is it our fault?

Every student wants to be able to learn easily, and when learning doesn't come easy, they think, "I don't want to do that, thank you very much." It's our job as homeschooling parents to find tools and services that will help our children and to make them want to keep trying.

When You Think There's a Problem

As a parent, you're with your children all day, and you're most likely to be the first to realize your child might have a learning challenge. You'll no doubt get well-meaning advice from friends: "Oh, children learn differently," or, "Just wait and see."

The truth is that for some challenges, such as dyslexia, waiting will not help. If you think your child has a learning problem, don't wait to get help. Get your child evaluated, and then seek out services and resources. It'll save you both a lot of heartache and struggle.

In public school, children with learning disabilities are often pushed through the system. They hear things like:

"Try harder."

"Don't be lazy."

"He's just unmotivated."

"She needs to learn to pay attention."

This can be true in our homeschooling, too. We must remember that our children will each have unique challenges and strengths. No child is less than or defective. Every child is designed by God, for God.

What should we require of our homeschooling students? To teach them to do what we believe each one can do, and to do that well.

Homeschooling a Child with Learning Difficulties

Recently I attended a workshop on learning challenges by Joyce Pickering from the Shelton School in Dallas, Texas. Here are some practical tips I picked up. Feel free to try them. They should work with all our kids.

Teach patience. Teach your child the "waiting" position: sitting on the floor, legs crossed, hands on knees.

Teach turns. "I'm going to show you something. This is my turn, and soon it will be your turn."

Teach preparation. Slow kids down, prepare them, and get them ready to learn.

Teach healthy eating. High protein diets—and diets that limit carbs and sugar—can often help children with learning disabilities.

Teach routine. Routine is a gift to our children. For example, a bedtime routine clues their bodies in that they need to get ready to sleep.

I am thankful that I have found great therapists to help my children who have learning challenges. Therapy shouldn't be seen as something that takes time away from homeschooling. Instead, look at it as a vital part of your child's education that will help him or her to learn better and easier in the future.

I've also discovered the greatest tool that I use to help me with my children is patience. Not all children will be ready by age six, and that's okay. As I look to God for wisdom and seek help for my children, I've see a lot of improvement. To see my children grow in their love for learning excites me, because I know they will have greater success in the future.

Homeschooling a Child with a Strong Will

I used to laugh when my mother-in-law, Darlyne, told me how my husband was a strong-willed child. That was until our daughter turned out to be exactly like her dad.

Darlyne used to tell stories about when John was a baby. She said he'd crawl to the nearest electrical outlet and try to stick his finger in it. She'd tell him no, gently slap his hand, pull him away, and yet he'd return. She'd do that over and over, trying to teach him. She'd turn his attention to something else, trying to distract him. Finally, she'd give up, and she'd have to cover the outlet.

"But I learned as he grew that his strong will benefited him in the long run," Darlyne told me. I believed her.

As a scrawny high schooler, John was told he'd never make it in the Marines. So he joined. He not only made it, but he graduated top of his class. In the military, he stayed true to God, even when alcohol and women were readily available. All his life, John has lived as a man of honor and excels in his work. His strong will has taken him far.

This, of course, wasn't comforting as I dealt with my own strong-willed child. Leslie was a sweet baby doll her first year of life, but things changed once she turned two years old. She'd have tantrums if she didn't get her way. She'd hide behind me and refuse to talk when people approached her. If I gave her a blue cup, she wanted the red one. If I offered a cookie, she'd want a cracker, and vice versa. Each day was a battle—my will against hers. There were days I loved my child but didn't like her that much.

The parenting class Growing Kids God's Way helped a lot. I can't remember everything that was taught, but here are some things that I stuck to along the way.

- **I NARROWED MY DAUGHTER'S CHOICES:** Instead of offering a blue cup and her demanding a green one, I'd offer both colors and let her pick from those two. Of course, she'd then want the red cup, but I didn't give in. She had to pick between the two. This worked for clothes, snacks, and other things. I'd still give my daughter a choice, but I'd limit those choices. After a while, the battles stopped. She soon understood that I wouldn't give in to her whines.

- **I PREPARED HER FOR INTERACTION:** If we were going to church, I'd explain possible things that could happen, such as people introducing themselves or commenting on her pretty dress. I'd role-play the correct response with her. And then I'd reward her when she responded correctly. I soon discovered that with some instruction, my daughter not only responded correctly, but she soon came out of her shell and became a chatterbox.

- **I STOOD BY MY WORD:** Even if my daughter disagreed or challenged me, I didn't give in. I learned that giving in was showing her that a bad attitude would get her what she wanted—and that's not what I wanted to reward. Once that no longer worked, she discovered that behaving well got her the best results.

- **I FOCUSED HER STRONG WILL ON POSITIVE THINGS:** Academics, piano, and friendships—I gave her the tools to excel in things she was good at, using her will as a benefit. And when the going got tough, she dug in.

- **I FOCUSED ON FILLING HER LOVE TANK:** My daughter is a quality time and gifts person. She gets excited when I bring her a pack of gum or her favorite lip gloss from the store. She loves when I take her to coffee or when we go to lunch. As we spent time face to face, my daughter opened up about everything she was dealing with. She even confessed to some areas that she struggled with. I discovered that she wasn't as strong as she liked everyone to believe. When I filled her love tank, her will weakened, and we built a bond that has remained for years.

Those are a few simple things that helped me. As the months passed, my daughter's attitude changed, and I enjoyed her more and more. I also discovered her strong will did help her excel. When her peers were still in college, she already had her degree and moved on to mission work. At twenty-two years old, she lived with two roommates in the Czech Republic, and she shared her faith with teens in a place where ninety percent of people are unchurched. Her will pushed her through four years of college before she was twenty-one. Her will has helped her adjust to a new country and find ways to push through spiritual barriers in this former Communist country.

Looking back, I'm appreciative that God made her who she is. With a will like hers, she'll be able to do many things for God's glory! I can't wait to see what else God has in store.

Our Prayer

Lord, thank You for our strong-willed children. They have a valiant sense of strength. I'm honored to have the opportunity to instill valuable character traits in them. Guide my patience, my parenting tools, and my own sense of strength. Remind me that You've given my child a strong will for Your great purposes in this world. Help me to trust in whatever those purposes are. In Jesus name, Amen.

Chapter Twenty-Three

•••••••••••••••••••••••••••••

Homeschooling Adopted Children

Tricia

As a wife, a mom, a sinner-saved-by-grace, and a servant of God, I have peace knowing God has a plan for my life. That He's always had a plan. And that He's here to guide me to His path for me. This is one of my favorite verses: "All the days ordained for me were written in your book before one of them came to be," (Psalm 139:16).

I look to this verse because I need the reminder that God isn't finished with me yet. I'm thankful I'm a work-in-progress. I'm happy to put (and keep) my life in God's hands. Yet, when I think of my kids' lives, I want to be more of an active participant. I forget God has all my children's days planned, too. For some reason, I try to wrangle the responsibility out of His hands and put it into mine. I try to figure out the best path for my kids and then pray and ask God to help me achieve it.

When my husband and I started the process of adopting our first two children out of the foster care system, they were just two and five years old. I knew that we'd have challenges, but my mind never swayed from my educational choice to homeschool them. After all, I'd been a homeschooling mom for twenty years! I homeschooled our oldest three from preschool through high school, and it was a wonderful experience. Yet homeschooling my adopted kids didn't happen as easily, or as quickly, as I'd thought.

Homeschooling Alyssa from preschool was no problem. We adopted her as a newborn from a private placement. Yet adopting from the foster care system, and homeschooling our other, now six, adopted children, has been a different story.

Right away, I discovered my children's numerous issues, the tragic results of abuse and neglect. These issues were more complex than I could handle. I knew how to be a mom, even a homeschooling mom, but my children needed behavioral, speech, and occupational therapy. Within a few weeks, I realized I needed help outside our home ... lots of it!

With the help of our social worker, my husband and I found the best resources for our new kids. We found amazing therapists who worked with us on bonding and caring for these children with past issues.

I have to admit there were moments when I felt like a traitor for still calling myself a homeschooling mom, especially when two out of three of my kids who were still school age were away from the home for a large part of the day. But God has reminded me that this was part of His plan ... even when it wasn't part of mine. He knew before they were born what they would need in order to heal. He knew the people who would help them and guide them. He brought co-laborers to help me with the process.

My goal has been for these children to find healing and for us to come to the place where we could be a happy, healthy, and thriving homeschooling family. Yet God has shown me that sometimes being the best homeschool mom means finding the right help for my children in different seasons of our lives.

Here are a few things that I learned as we have added seven adopted children into our family, six of whom were from the foster care system. I hope that they will bless you and help you to find more freedom to think outside the typical homeschool box when trying to ascertain what's best for your children.

Homeschooling should never be a label we wear to the sacrifice of our children's needs

Homeschooling is a wonderful choice, but there might be some situations where there is an even better choice—perhaps if you have a child with special needs. If your child needs special education, or more help than you give, then it might not be the right season to homeschool that child. And that's okay. Don't feel bad about it. Your child is more valuable than your homeschooling label.

Homeschooling is about finding God's plan for our children's lives and helping them thrive within it. I needed the reminder that God isn't finished with my children yet. I'm thankful they are works-in-progress, just as I am. And I'm learning to happily put (and keep) their lives in His hands.

Our state had a say

The State of Arkansas told me that homeschooling foster children was not allowed. Even though we had an adoption plan for Casey and Bella, they were considered foster children until the adoption was final. For us, this took just over six months. This also held true with our four more recently adopted daughters. Maria, Lauren, Jordan, and Florentina, were already school-aged when we were going through the adoption process, we were required to keep them in public school until their adoption was final.

We used private school to start

Because of all she'd dealt with in her past, our six-year-old daughter Bella was considered a special needs child. Since I couldn't homeschool her while she was still in foster care, I found a wonderful private school for special needs kids. The teachers at this new school were godly, wonderful people who poured into her life. They knew how to handle her unique needs, and they cared for her so tenderly. We saw Bella grow and heal in her time there. It was a great schooling choice for us.

We tried not to change too much, too soon.

When we Casey moved into our home, at two-and-a-half he'd been in an all-day daycare. I was used to having my children at home, and it seemed unnatural to me to take him to daycare for most of the day. Instead of daycare—with the help of our social worker—I found an all-day center where Casey could get all of his therapy (speech, occupational, and physical). It took a lot of self-talk to remind myself this was okay. Casey needed the therapy. It also helped him to keep things familiar for a while. To him, going to preschool all day was normal, even though it didn't feel that way for me. Gradually, I kept him home more and more until home became the familiar and safe place. After nine months Casey didn't need as much therapy, and he was home full-time!

I had to ax the guilt

Of course, making these schooling choices for my kids meant I had to ax the guilt. It was okay that my daughter was being educated outside of the home. I wasn't compromising by enrolling her in school. Instead of feeling guilty, I looked at this school choice as something we were doing for a season. Casey received the therapy help he needed and Bella did too ... in a Christian classroom. When this season came to a close, Bella and Casey came home, and we were all ready for it.

We took things slowly

I'm so glad now that I took things slowly. I realize the most important thing was that we all had time to adjust. Bringing new children into a home takes a lot of adjustment. Homeschooling them does, too.

Just because you believe homeschooling is the best choice doesn't mean it's the best choice, today, for your adopted kids. Seek God and ask Him to help you with your children's unique paths. Just like homeschool curriculum, your adopted child's journey to homeschooling can be tailored to fit their needs.

The best way to homeschool adopted kids is in a way that meets their unique needs and allows them to adjust to your family and your homeschooling lifestyle over time.

Our Prayer

Lord, I know You designed each one of us, and You knew who we were designed to be from the foundation of the world. Forgive me, Lord, when I've been discouraged because my children have designs different than what I wished for or wanted. Who am I to think that my imaginary designs are better than Your infinitely wise and tangible ones? Lord, give me wisdom and patience. Also, give me answers from people who are trained to offer help. Let me not be too prideful to ask for help either. Thank you, Lord, for all Your provision. In Jesus' name, Amen.

Chapter Twenty-Four

. . . .

If Nothing Else, Remember This ...

Tricia & Kristi

There you have it. We've poured our hearts into giving you the best homeschooling advice we can muster in this pretty little book. Whether you're just starting out and feeling like you're drinking from a fire hydrant, or if you've been at this for a while and just needed some extra encouragement, our prayer is that between these pages, you've found a few nuggets that will be a blessing to you and your homeschool.

There's no way to provide all the information you need for your homeschooling journey in one book, but our hope is that we were able to encourage you, give you confidence, and help you find answers in the midst of your struggle. Also, know that no homeschooling mom ever feels as if she's arrived. We all hit the proverbial wall at times. Sometimes we just need a little refreshment and perspective to break through. Both of us continually seek advice and inspiration from others. We all need it. Think of it this way: we are modeling for our kids our love for learning and growing when we continue to learn new things and explore new ways of homeschooling.

After pouring out all that we have to give, we want to leave you with one last thought—that if nothing else remember this piece of advice:

No matter what struggles or joys you're having on this homeschooling journey, all your hard work will come down to one moment. That's the moment when our children stand before the Lord at the end of their days here on earth. Jesus is not going to give them a math test or ask to see their college entrance essays. At that moment, they will hear one of two things. They will either hear, "Well done, good and faithful servant," or "I'm sorry, I don't know you."

> **Our goal is to do everything in our power to ensure our children know the Truth, so they can walk with their Lord all their days and stand before him, redeemed and unashamed, in glory.**

If you can keep your focus on that, if you can always remember why you're doing what you're doing, even those challenging days and seasons will be endurable.

Yes, math, grammar, and history facts are important, but nothing is more important than teaching your child what a relationship with Christ is all about.

Yes, discovering your child's learning styles, talents, and interest are important, but teaching them that their sole purpose on earth is to glorify God and serve Him forever is key.

Yes, protecting our children from ungodly influences helps them better grow into men and women who will know how to protect their own minds and their own hearts, but it's just as important to remind them that God put us on this earth not to hide away but to love and serve others. When we write out our priorities for our homeschool, we need to make sure these higher goals are on the top of the list.

Don't Sweat all the Little Stuff

Let us offer one last bit of encouragement: all the little stuff that we so often worry and stress about is just that ... little stuff. If tomorrow you work all day and never complete one assignment but you pray with your children, you read from God's Word, and you share the love of God with others, consider it a success. Success in this world is different than success in God's eyes, and if you and your kids learn just one thing on this homeschooling journey, let it be that.

Matthew 6:33-34 says,

> But seek first His kingdom and His righteousness, and all these things will be given to you as well. Therefore do not worry about tomorrow, for tomorrow will worry about itself. Each day has enough trouble of its own.

Can I get an Amen on that? We will have troubles and worries during our homeschool journeys, but we are to seek Him first. Trust that Jesus will show up. He will give you the strength that you need.

Remember how we started this book with our Indiana Jones moment—that big step of faith that we take each day we homeschool? We want to end with another story about a step of faith.

There is a story in the Bible about a man named Peter who also took a big step of faith. In Matthew fourteen, we read about Jesus walking up to the boat that the disciples are on during a storm. They were all afraid. Yet Peter, bold, impetuous, and faithful Peter, stepped out of the boat and walked on water. But here's the kicker that we always have to remind ourselves of.

When Peter took His eyes off Jesus and focused on the waves, he started to sink.

Just like Peter, we have to keep our eyes on the Lord. There will be storms and hard crazy rock the boat kind of days in your homeschool. That we can pretty much guarantee. However, the more we remind ourselves to focus on the Lord and remember that final moment we are preparing our kids for, the more you'll find His peace that "transcends all understanding" (Philippians 4:7).

The storms will come. The doubts will swirl around your mind like a hurricane, but you will find success if you keep your eyes on Jesus. And as you focus on Him, your children will learn to focus on Him, too. And your family members' lives—and eternity—will be forever transformed for good. They will be forever transformed for God, and for His glory, too. And isn't that what homeschooling is all about?

May the Lord bless you, your family, and your homeschool.

Blessings and joy!

Resources

We hope you were blessed by all that we shared with you in this book. All of these resources, printables, and more can be found at: www.thehomeschoolbasics.com We have a special resource page for you there that you can access with the password:

HOMESCHOOLROCKS

Coming Soon…Your Thriving Homeschool: The Podcast!

Highlighted Books

Prayers that Changed History: From Christopher Columbus to Helen Keller, How God Used 25 People to Change the World by Tricia Goyer

Balanced: Finding Center as a Work-at-Home Mom by Tricia Goyer

Walk it Out: The Radical Result of Living God's Word One Step at a Time by Tricia Goyer

Sanity Savers for Moms by Kristi Clover

Courses

Ultimate Homeschool Organization Course: www.HomeschoolOrganization.com

Homeschool Basics: The Course … coming in 2018

Connect with Us

Find Tricia at TriciaGoyer.com

Join her Tricia Goyer Newsletter by texting
FOLLOWTRICIA at 22828

Pinterest: www.Pinterest.com/TriciaGoyer

Facebook: www.Facebook.com/AuthorTriciaGoyer

Facebook Group for Avid Readers of Christian Fiction:
www.facebook.com/groups/AvidChristFicReaders

Twitter: www.Twitter.com/TriciaGoyer

Instagram: www.Instagram.com/TriciaGoyer

Find Kristi at KristiClover.com

Join her Simply Joyful Newsletter and get her book,
Sanity Savers for Moms, FREE!
Just go to www.KristiClover.com/join

Kristi's homeschool videos can be found on her
YouTube channel at www.KristiClover.tv

The Simply Joyful Podcast:
www.simplyjoyfulpodcast.com

Facebook: KristiClover.com/Facebook — Don't miss her
"Live" #HomeschoolHacks Videos Fridays @12pm PST

The Simply Joyful Facebook Group:
www.facebook.com/groups/simplyjoyful

Pinterest: www.KristiClover.com/Pinterest

For information about all the websites and curriculum mentioned go to:

www.thehomeschoolbasics.com